C000085847

CAMBRIDGESHIRE
Strange but True

ROBERT HALLIDAY

SUTTON PUBLISHING

First published in the United Kingdom in 2007 by
Sutton Publishing Limited · Phoenix Mill
Thrupp · Stroud · Gloucestershire · GL5 2BU

British Library Cataloguing in Publication Data
A catalogue record for this book is available from the British Library.

ISBN 978-0-7509-4059-7

Typeset in Joanna 11/13pt.
Typesetting and origination by
Sutton Publishing Limited.
Printed and bound in England.

This book is dedicated to my aunt
Eileen Halliday
of Port Washington, New York, USA,
in grateful thanks for her constant help, support and encouragement over many years.

CAMBRIDGESHIRE
Strange
BUT True

CONTENTS

INTRODUCTION AND ACKNOWLEDGEMENTS

This work tries to throw some new light on Cambridgeshire (which now includes the historic county of Huntingdonshire and the Soke of Peterborough), and hopes to give the reader some information on some of the better-known, but also some of the lesser-known and more frequently overlooked, themes in the county's history.

Historical trends, people and events cannot be ignored, as they continue to affect Cambridgeshire in many ways, both tangible and otherwise. The past is not static: historic buildings and institutions have been changed and adapted. The county's oldest secular houses – the School of Pythagoras at Cambridge and Hemingford Grey Manor House – have undergone many changes, yet they still possess vitality: one as a part of a Cambridge college, the other as the house of an author whose works are read and enjoyed by many.

This book has its origins in my childhood in Cambridge, where the many old buildings and stories of past events awakened my interest in history and in seeking out information about the past. To this end I owe an incalculable debt to Rock Road Branch Library in Cambridge, where regular visits to the local history shelves nurtured this interest, making me aware of the region's historical and archaeological potential, and helping me to understand it.

Many people have helped in the preparation of this book. Thanks are due to the staff of The Cambridgeshire Collection in Cambridge Central Library, in particular to Fiona Parish for her unstinting help in locating and assembling photographs and illustrations, and to Chris Jakes, the local studies librarian, for continual and patient help and assistance with a wide variety of enquiries. Thanks are also due to Bob Burn-Murdoch of the Norris Museum at St Ives for assistance with a variety of enquiries on Huntingdonshire local history and an excellent photograph of the Bury Fen Bandy Team; to Olive Main and Kelvin Davis of Stilton for illustrations and information about the annual cheese-rolling; to Diana Boston of Hemingford Grey for providing a most informative guided tour of her house and for answering further queries; to Terry Holloway of the Marshall Group of Companies for photographs of Concorde; to Jim Potter of Balsham for photographs of and information on his wonderful hedge maze; to Tom and Anne Wood for photographs of the Witcham Pea Shooting Championships; and to Steve Macaulay of the Cambridgeshire Archaeological Field Unit for photographs of earthworks and information on related subjects.

Other people who deserve thanks include Mary Boyall, a friendly and helpful tour guide at Peterborough Cathedral, for information on the building and its surroundings; Jeff Burt of Molesworth for allowing me access to what little remains of the pet cemetery; David Cullum of the Barnwell and Fen Ditton Local History Society for information on that area of Cambridgeshire; Joan Denehy for observations on St Mark's Church at Friday Bridge; Jan Ellam of Balsham for information on Balsham's Plough Monday celebrations; Philip Hensman of Great St Mary's Church, Cambridge, for information on the building; Dr

The Minnie Mice, one of the best fancy-dress cheese-rolling teams at Stilton in 2006.
(*Stilton Community Association*)

Nicholas James, the President of the Cambridge Antiquarian Society, for information on Cambridge topography; Terry Kavanagh of the St Radegund pub for information on the King Street Run; the staff at Madingley Hall for information on the pet memorials there; Duncan MacAndrew for pointing out a Wild Man at St Botolph's Church; Tinch Minter for some insights on the name Cambourne; Meryl Moore for information on the stained glass at Swaffham Prior; Alan Murdie and Adriana Sascombe-Welles for hints and insights; Maureen Watson, the curator of Whittlesey Museum, and her assistants for information on Whittlesey; and Simon Fletcher, Matilda Pearce, Michelle Tilling and Jane Hutchings of Sutton Publishing for their help and support throughout the preparation of this book.

1 ODD LIVES

It would be impossible to list all the famous and unusual characters who have lived in Cambridgeshire, but there are some unfairly underrated people who deserve to be better known.

Robert Scarlett

Peterborough was home to Robert Scarlett, also known as Old Scarlett, the country's most famous gravedigger. Born in 1496, he became parish clerk and sexton of St John the Baptist's Church, and then sexton to the abbey, where in 1536 he buried Queen Catherine of Aragon. He continued as sexton during the Reformation and the Dissolution of the Monasteries, when the abbey church became the cathedral. In 1572 St John's parish registers record a payment of 8s for a gown 'to Scarlett, being a poor old man, and rising oft in the night to toll the bell for sick persons, the weather being grievous, and in consideration of his good service'. He was still performing his duties at the age of 91 (probably in a supervisory capacity) when he was in charge of the burial of Mary Queen of Scots in 1587. He died seven years later. Living through nearly the entire Tudor Age, Scarlett buried two generations of Peterborough residents. Evidently he made a great impression on those who knew him: his memorial was placed so that it dominated the interior of the cathedral's west end, where a large mural portrait still stands above a verse epitaph describing him as 'second to none for strength and sturdy limb'.

Mikepher Alphery

Woolley once had a Russian Rector: Mikiforko Olfer'yev syn Grigor'yev, whose name was anglicised to Mikepher Alphery. His story still seems relevant today. In 1601 Tsar Boris Godunov of Russia entrusted four young Russians to John Merrick, the English Ambassador, for education in England, hoping they would eventually return home to benefit their mother country. Mikepher studied at Clare College and converted to the Church of England, being ordained a priest in 1615. Meanwhile, the Russian Embassy had demanded their countrymen's return, though they did not wish to go: they probably had little memory of their homeland, and Mikepher, having abandoned the Orthodox faith, would have been subject to ill-treatment and persecution on returning home. An attempt was made to kidnap Mikepher. John Merrick then arranged a fruitless meeting with a Russian ambassador. When James I and the Privy Council heard about Mikepher they said it would be wrong to return him to Russia against his will, especially if he could not practise his religious beliefs there.

Mikepher had been appointed Rector of Woolley in 1608. He married an Englishwoman, and they had eight children. At the start of the Civil War his life was again disrupted when a troop of Parliamentary soldiers ejected him from church during a service and turned his family from the rectory. During the war Royalist ministers were expelled from Parliamentary areas and vice versa. Mikepher may have been attached to the Stuart monarchy that allowed him to stay in England. But village factions did use soldiers to settle

Ruins of Woolley Church. Passing out of use after the Second World War, as the village was virtually depopulated, the church was deliberately subjected to partial demolition by the ecclesiastical authorities. (*Author's collection*)

old scores; Mikepher's replacement was a local man, so anti-foreign prejudice may have played a part. For a week Mikepher and his family camped under a tree in the churchyard, perhaps to protest against their treatment and to embarrass those who had ejected them. He then preached at Easton, where members of his old congregation joined him. At the Restoration in 1660 he returned to Woolley, before retiring to his son's house in London. Some Alpherys lived in Warboys for another century, where they were said to be members of the Russian royal family. Evidently the romance of the family's story grew over the years.

David Culy

Nonconformist Christianity has always been popular in the Fens, but the region's only indigenous congregation were the Culimites, followers of David Culy. Born to descendants of French protestant refugees at Guyhirn, David was converted in 1687 after hearing Francis Holcroft, a local preacher. He began preaching in Guyhirn, and on 26 July 1693 forty of his followers formed their own church, which spread across the Fens. David was called

Isleham Free Church. In Pound Lane, this is the only standing place of worship that can demonstrate a direct connection with the Culimites: the first chapel on this site was established by members of David Culy's Soham congregation, although it was wholly rebuilt in 1808. It later became a Baptist Chapel, and is now a free church. (*Author's collection*)

'The Bishop of Guyhirn' which we can only hope amused him, as, like all Nonconformists, he would have rejected hierarchical church organisation. Examined in court at Wisbech, David successfully defended his ministry. In an effort to silence him he was press-ganged onto a ship at King's Lynn, where he sung hymns until the crew put him ashore at Great Yarmouth.

After David's wife, Anne Delahoi, died in 1697 there are vague indications that he was linked with another woman from his congregation. Although there is no certain evidence, this may have caused dissension among his followers, as in 1699 his Soham followers seceded from his leadership. But his teaching spread into Lincolnshire, and he moved to Billinghay. Here he died in 1725, when he had over 700 followers, including 100 at Guyhirn.

Culimites met in each other's houses: they did not open a chapel until 1751, on the South Brink at Wisbech, and this may only have been a converted house. His followers eventually dispersed or joined the Baptists, but even in the nineteenth century the expressions Culimite and Nonconformist were still synonymous in the Fens.

Jane Stuart

Jane Stuart was a mystery woman who appeared in Wisbech in 1688, the year that James II, Britain's last Stuart king, was expelled from the throne. Standing on the town bridge, where people traditionally waited for farm work, her demeanour set her apart. Asked if she could reap she said she could learn; taken to a farm she proved the most energetic and productive worker. She lodged in a cellar near the market, where she spun and sold cloth, saying 'she would not leave her cell and spinning to be Queen of England'.

After the Civil War the British royal family had sheltered at the French court, where it was rumoured that Jane had been the result of a liaison between the young James and a French lady-in-waiting. Jane said she was leaving London with her fiancé at the time of James II's overthrow, but their coach crashed, killing her husband-to-be. A loyal member of the Wisbech Quaker congregation (James II had been tolerant of Quakers) she evaded questions about her origin. However, widely repeated stories continued to circulate: that

Jane Stuart's grave in the cemetery of the Friends' Meeting House at Wisbech. (*Author's collection*)

people visiting her unexpectedly found her reading the New Testament in the original Greek; that she went to Scotland in 1715 when James II's son landed there to try to reclaim the throne; that a stately coach had once arrived in Wisbech and its aristocratic owner had roamed the town asking about Jane, who hid herself in the cellar until his departure. On her death in 1742 Jane was buried in the cemetery behind the Wisbech Quaker Meeting House on the North Brink. Although Quakers disliked elaborate gravestones, the congregation paid for a headstone marked, 'Jane Stuart, died 1742, aged 88 years', an enigmatic memorial to an enigmatic life.

Elizabeth Woodcock

Elizabeth Woodcock's ordeal still conjures romantic images in her native Impington. On Saturday 2 February 1799, she was riding her horse Tinker home from Cambridge through a particularly heavy snowstorm when a light startled him. Elizabeth dismounted, while Tinker galloped across the fields. She followed him for half a mile, then, cold and exhausted, sheltered under a thorn thicket. By Sunday morning a snow cave had formed over her, and her legs were too numb to move. She tied her handkerchief to a branch and

Contemporary engraving of Elizabeth Woodcock in her snow cave. (Cambridgeshire Collection, Cambridge Central Library)

pushed it through a hole in the snow to signal to passers-by. Elizabeth spent eight days in her snow cave, not feeling tedium or boredom, but listening to nearby church bells and passing travellers, while praying and thinking of her family. Her husband and friends looked for her, searching a gypsy camp on the suspicion that gypsies had murdered or kidnapped her, but to no avail.

On Sunday 10 February, William Muncey, a local farmer, saw a strange object in the snow. Going to investigate, he found Elizabeth's handkerchief. Spotting Elizabeth through a hole in the snow, William did not speak, but rushed to the road where he met two people: one returned to Elizabeth, while the other accompanied him to summon help. Luckily, Thomas Okes, a Cambridge surgeon, was visiting Impington; he took her home and

An obelisk marks the site of Elizabeth Woodcock's snow cave. The height of the pillar is the same as the depth of the snow. (*Author's collection*)

provided medical care. Within hours people were coming to see Elizabeth, many bringing brandy (a drink she enjoyed). Thomas Okes wrote a book about her ordeal which went through three editions in three months. Despite hopes for her recovery she died in July. The parish register caustically suggests this was partly due to the brandy well-wishers brought her. In 1849 local farmers called French and Saunders (no relation to the television personalities) had an obelisk placed on the site of her snow cave.

Abraham Cawston

Abraham Westerman Cawston, 'The Chippenham Croesus', caused a great stir in Cambridgeshire after claiming to have acquired great wealth. Born in 1800, Abraham was the son of John Cawston, a maltster at Chippenham, who sent him to Shrewsbury public school at the age of 15. The headmaster of Shrewsbury wrote to John Cawston saying that, although an excellent scholar, Abraham lived a remarkably extravagant lifestyle, and had once offered to change a ten-pound banknote for coins. This seemed unusual, even at a school for boys from wealthy and aristocratic families. Abraham told his father he could say nothing until New Year's Day. He then told him how he had shared the Shrewsbury stagecoach with an elderly man with a foreign accent. They had had a lengthy conversation in which they had disagreed on everything. A few days later Abraham had received an invitation to meet the man, who was called Don Gaspar De Quintilla. Having realised that Abraham's views were correct, Don Gaspar wished they could be friends. Don Gaspar showed great generosity, writing a will naming Abraham as sole beneficiary, on condition that he kept this secret until the start of 1817. Soon afterwards Don Gaspar had died, and Abraham received deeds from Mr Stanistreet, a Liverpool solicitor, giving details of world-wide interests worth over £500,000. Abraham had buried these, but was not allowed to say where.

The Fortunate Youth, as Abraham was called, became a national celebrity. Relatives and friends loaned him over £1,000 to cover his expenses until his fortune could be realised. His brother William was enrolled at Cambridge University. The Cawstons were courted by tradesmen, financiers and even society figures. They entered into negotiations to buy Houghton Hall in Norfolk and acquire interests in parliamentary boroughs to nominate MPs who they hoped would obtain them a peerage.

One evening Abraham entertained some wealthy new friends, and he held forth on the wine, insisting that it came from his Sicilian estates. One guest noticed that the corks were stamped by a London wine merchant. When approached the wine merchant denied knowledge of Abraham. Mr Stanistreet was then contacted: he too denied knowledge of Abraham and Don Gaspar. The Morning Chronicle warned of a fraudster at large. While Abraham's supporters threatened to sue for libel, Abraham fled England, claiming urgent business on his Spanish estates. The bubble burst in December, when Abraham's supporters found themselves rather poorer. Apparently, Abraham had developed an attachment to a young noblewoman, and thought the story of Don Gaspar would persuade her to marry him.

Two plays about 'The Fortunate Youth' were staged in London, in which, respectively, he was called 'Abraham Gullem' and the 'Mandeville Munchausen'.

Abraham apparently escaped prosecution. He was later admitted into holy orders and became tutor to the children of a relative near Bury St Edmunds, where he died in 1861.

Edward Purkis Frost

Edward Purkis Frost of West Wratting Hall was an unusual aviation pioneer. Born in 1842, between 1869 and 1877 Edward spent £1,000 building an 'ornithopter': a machine which would fly by flapping three pairs of wings, the largest, copied from a crow, with a 30ft span. Weighing 600lb, and requiring a 5½hp engine to move the wings, it was far too heavy to fly. Edward must have anticipated this: he probably made his ornithopter to study the movement of the wings, or in the hope that others might develop his ideas.

At the end of the nineteenth century he met Frederick Hutchinson of Trinity Hall College and a certain C. D'Esterre. They made a 3ft ornithopter from light steel whose wings flapped 350 times a minute. In 1902 they developed this into a full-size machine, powered by a motorcycle engine, with 8ft wings that flapped 100 times a minute; when suspended in a frame it rose two feet.

Edward's experiments were rendered obsolete by the Wright brothers in 1903. Nevertheless, he remained a respected member of Britain's flying community, at one point being elected president of the Royal Aeronautical Society. He wrote books demonstrating the compatibility of science and religion and ways to prevent war. Asked about his flight experiments he said they 'opened my eyes to the wonder of nature to an extent which could not have been arrived at in any other way. It is a beautiful study.'

Edward Purkis Frost's last ornithopter, built in 1903. (*Cambridgeshire Collection, Cambridge Central Library*)

Edward Purkis Frost and his homemade wings. (*Cambridgeshire Collection, Cambridge Central Library*)

Nicholas Saunderson

Some Cambridgeshire people have overcome disabilities to achieve distinction. Nicholas Saunderson lost his eyesight to smallpox in 1683, at the age of one. Yet he showed great aptitude for learning, and moved to Cambridge at the age of 24. Although not a member of the university, he lived at Christ's College, where he became a respected teacher. Aged 27 he was elected Lucasian Professor of Mathematics – the post previously held by Isaac Newton – partly through Queen Anne's support. (Interestingly, the present Lucasian Professor is Stephen Hawking.) An expert flute player, Nicholas had an acute ear and could judge a room's size and his place in it from sound vibrations. When given some ancient coins of doubtful authenticity he could distinguish the forgeries from the genuine antiquities by touch; of all the academics who examined them, his conclusions were the most accurate.

Henry Fawcett

Henry Fawcett was born in 1833. He graduated as Seventh Wrangler and became a Fellow of Trinity Hall. Blinded by a shooting accident at 25, Fawcett determined that this would make no difference to his life. He became Professor of Political Economy at Cambridge and played an important role in movements to modernise the university and admit women. As the first blind MP he led the Liberal Party's radical wing. Later appointed Postmaster

General, Fawcett introduced the parcel post and postal orders. He lived at 18 Brookside in Cambridge; on his death in 1883 he was buried in Trumpington churchyard. At the time Fawcett was said to be the most popular man in England after Gladstone.

Bessie Jones

Elizabeth, or 'Bessie', Jones accomplished much, despite being left deaf and blind by measles at the age of two. Descended from Jewish immigrants, her father was a successful Cambridge dentist. Bessie communicated with a finger alphabet which she devised with her family. William Whewell, the Master of Trinity College, was impressed by the sensitive and caring way she joined in family life. An expert at needlework and embroidery, Bessie made a decorated purse for Queen Victoria. She is commemorated in St Paul's Church in Cambridge by a stained-glass window showing Holman Hunt's *Light of The World*.

Walter Cornelius

Walter Cornelius was an immigrant who successfully adapted to Cambridgeshire life. When his native Latvia was occupied by the Soviet Union he fled across the Baltic with some partisans who came to England and were given shelter at Sibson airfield. Walter stayed in the area, working as a lifeguard at Peterborough swimming pool. In 1966 he became world sausage-eating champion after consuming twenty-three in ten minutes. A year later he performed his strongman act on *Opportunity Knocks* (British television's first and longest-running talent show).

His eccentric stunts included an attempt to fly over the River Nene from Brierley's supermarket with a pair of home-made wings – he promptly fell into the water. More successful tricks included skipping with a 48lb chain for 90 minutes, pushing a double-

Walter Cornelius, the Peterborough Strongman, demonstrating his strength by having a concrete slab broken over his head, 1968. Don't try this at home, folks! (*Pathé Archive*)

decker bus half a mile with his head, and eating 3½lb of raw onions in two minutes and two seconds (on separate occasions) under monitored conditions, to set world records, as well as pushing a pea up Castor Hill and a cannonball a mile (on both occasions with his nose)! There are jokes about the confused would-be record breaker who tried to drive a bus over a motorcycle: Walter's last stunt, in 1982, was to attempt to drive a bus over fourteen parked motorcycles at a local fête.

In September 1983 Walter failed to turn up for work. He had died of heart failure at the age of 60. Although he had no family in Peterborough, his many friends and admirers paid for his funeral. Reluctant to speak about his early life in Latvia, Walter had adapted to Cambridgeshire life with great success, and was genuinely proud to be awarded British citizenship in 1971. His lifestyle was simple: living in a caravan, he gave all the money raised by his stunts and acts to charity.

Charlie Cavey

Charlie Cavey has devised one of the region's most unusual musical entertainments by busking from a cast-iron litter bin. Many buskers have plied their trade on the streets of Cambridge, but some years ago Charlie decided to refine his act by acquiring a metal dustbin and performing from that. A familiar sight in the Bridge Street area of Cambridge, his act inevitably attracts a widespread and bemused audience. His repertoire includes songs by Elvis Presley and Tom Jones, as well as more recent pop songs. I first saw him performing from his dustbin in 2002, and stopped to enquire about his act. A few seconds afterwards somebody stopped me to ask about his choice of material. Showing my age I said he was in the correct place for the performance of much present-day pop music. It transpired that the scene was being filmed for the regional television news, and for the rest of the year I was approached by people who said they saw me on TV talking to a dustbin!

Charlie Cavey, one of Cambridge's more unconventional buskers, performing on his usual pitch in Bridge Street before an incredulous audience. (*Author's collection*)

Snowy Farr

Snowy Farr from Oakington is a well-known Cambridge charity fund-raiser. Born Walter Farr in Longstanton in 1919, he became a road mender for the County Council in the Oakington area and was one of the last members of that profession. He decorated his cart with banners, and wore a top hat when on duty.

Approaching retirement, Snowy decided to raise money for charity by making a pre-Christmas trip with his cart to Cambridge's Market Hill where he pretended to be Father Christmas. He proved a popular success, partly since he bore more than a little resemblance to the character he was impersonating. When cycling home a family thought he so resembled Father Christmas on his rounds that they asked him to come in and meet their children. Snowy decided to continue fund-raising for charity and took a cat and some white mice to enliven his cart. Over the following years his animal friends grew into a small portable menagerie, with a cockerel, a duck, budgerigars, pigeons, rabbits, guinea pigs and more mice than anybody could count; he trained his cat to sit on his top hat, and let some mice run around the brim. He concentrated on raising money for the blind and by 1995 Snowy had paid for twenty-two guide dogs. By then his popularity was such that a local campaign was started to place him on the Queen's Birthday Honours list, leading to his being awarded the MBE. On arrival at Buckingham Palace Prince Charles immediately recognised Snowy from his own Cambridge student days. Snowy has even become something of an international celebrity: he has featured in the standard English-language

textbook in Italy, and after being mentioned on US television a letter from New Mexico simply addressed 'Snowy, Children's Animal Man, Cambridge' reached him through the international postal system without difficulty. By the end of the twentieth century he had raised more than £46,000 for Guide Dogs for the Blind and over £23,000 for Camsight (a local charity). Although the onset of old age has made Snowy's appearances in Cambridge less frequent, there can be no doubt that he is a true 'king of the road'.

Snowy Farr at his usual pitch on the corner of Market Hill and Petty Cury in Cambridge.
(*Cambridgeshire Collection, Cambridge Central Library*)

2 ALL THINGS WISE AND WONDERFUL

Cambridge University is undoubtedly the county's most famous institution and is known the world over as an academic paragon, producing vast resources of scholarship and expertise. The only historian to have provided an explanation of the university's origin was Roger of Wendover, a monk of St Albans Abbey, in his *Flowers Of History*. This records how, between 1208 and 1209, an Oxford student accidentally killed a woman and fled the town. In retaliation the town officials hanged three students with whom he lodged. This disrupted the university and many scholars fled Oxford, some going as far as Cambridge. There is no obvious explanation for this migration, as the towns are 150 miles apart. But John Grim, the Master of the Schools at Oxford, came from a Cambridgeshire family and may have decided to return home, taking some of his students with him.

At first Cambridge University owned no property: it was simply a group of masters and students who taught and studied together. Great St Mary's, the town's largest and most central church, became the focus of university activity, where meetings and lectures were held, and documents stored; students are still expected to live within 10 miles of the

The Old Schools building, Cambridge, the oldest purpose-built university headquarters in Britain.
(*Cambridgeshire Collection, Cambridge Central Library*)

The Senate House. (*Cambridgeshire Collection, Cambridge Central Library*)

church while in residence at Cambridge. It was only in 1359 that the university authorities decided to build a separate headquarters, The Schools Building, west of Great St Mary's, which was not completed until 1400. Over the following eighty years three more ranges were added to form a courtyard now known as The Old Schools, the oldest purpose-built university building in Britain. Apart from the colleges, this remained the only university building in Cambridge until 1722, when The Senate House was built opposite Great St Mary's as a venue for university ceremonies and events.

Cambridge University is well known for its colleges. Peterhouse, the oldest, was founded by Hugh de Balsham, Bishop of Ely, in 1280, and moved to its present site in Trumpington Street in 1284. Henry VI was personally responsible for establishing King's College in 1441. Robinson, the newest college, opened in 1976. The university now comprises thirty-one colleges.

After Henry VIII dissolved the monasteries he forced an Act of Parliament authorising the dissolution of all religious corporations, raising the possibility that Oxford and Cambridge universities would be closed. Members of both universities appealed to Henry and his last wife Catherine Parr, insisting that their academic capabilities were important for the country, while presenting cleverly audited accounts to show that colleges ran at a continual financial loss, implying that Henry would actually lose money if he seized their property. Henry eventually spared the universities, and even founded Trinity College. It remains Cambridge's largest and wealthiest college, although not through royal generosity, being an amalgamation of two earlier colleges, Michaelhouse and King's Hall.

Holding large landed endowments, many colleges are wealthier than the university itself. At no other university have colleges achieved the overwhelming importance they occupy at Oxford and Cambridge. All are run by 'Fellows', highly qualified graduates, most of whom hold posts as university lecturers or administrators.

All Cambridge students enrol at a college, and will live there (or on college property) for most of the time they pursue their studies. Students who pay for college lodgings, from their own funds or outside assistance, are called Pensioners (as they pay a pension for accommodation). Cambridge once admitted wealthy students as Fellow Commoners (as they paid for their 'Commons' or food). Paying high fees, they enjoyed privileged status, and often enjoyed themselves without attempting to study, yet they automatically received degrees (and priority at graduation ceremonies) to the great resentment of other students, who called Fellow Commoners 'empty bottles' (and vice versa). Poor students from humble backgrounds entered Cambridge as Sizars (because they received free sizes or bread and drink), who worked their way through college by performing menial tasks, such as waiting at meals. Many rose to become masters of their colleges or professors. Students coming to Cambridge as Sizars included the botanist and founder of scientific botany John Ray, the poets Samuel Taylor Coleridge and Oliver Goldsmith, the musician Orlando Gibbons and even Isaac Newton. These unfair and unequal positions have long since been abolished, but some colleges have revived the term Fellow Commoner for visiting scholars, while maintaining funds known as Sizarships to assist students in financial need.

Students are said to 'come up' to Cambridge, even though it is one of Britain's most low-lying cities, and to 'go down' at the finish of term or their studies. New students are called Freshmen (or 'Freshers' since the arrival of female students) and colleges hold Freshers' balls to help them to enter university life. On arrival they matriculate, a term derived from the Latin *matricula* meaning class list or register, on which students' names were enrolled. Students are said to 'keep' in a college, from an archaic usage of the word meaning to live or stay alive. Colleges contain 'Combination Rooms', where Fellows can meet, relax and socialise (or 'combine'). All College Fellows and academic staff are called dons, a medieval term of respect for a learned man (probably derived from the Latin *dominus* meaning master), although lacking any official meaning. The name has given rise to the adjective 'donnish' to describe an unworldly academic. Undergraduates were once called 'Sophisters' or 'Sophs', (from the Greek *sophos* meaning clever or wise) which was jokingly altered to 'Sophy Mores' or 'Sophomores' (using the Greek *mores*, foolish), to mean 'wise fools' or 'foolish wise men'.

A medieval student spent four years studying, and then discussed what he had learned with senior university members in a 'disputation'. After demonstrating knowledge and understanding he became a Bachelor of Arts, or BA. After three further years of study he became a Master (a Master of Arts or MA), when he ceremonially climbed steps (in Latin *gradus*) to be installed in a Master's Chair – hence the words 'graduate' and 'undergraduate'. All Masters originally spent at least two years teaching at Cambridge – they were known as 'Regents', a name still given to members of the university engaged in teaching – but requirements for obtaining an MA were simplified until all Cambridge graduates received one as a matter of course, since 1835 purchased by a £10 payment three years after graduation.

Cuthbert Holthouse of St John's College, the last student, in 1909, to be awarded a wooden spoon. Since then mathematics graduates, with the exception of Wranglers, have been listed alphabetically, so it is impossible to tell their relative results.
(*Cambridgeshire Collection, Cambridge Central Library*)

Degree examinations were not introduced until the eighteenth century. Early examinations were held in The Senate House, when Regents could come to deliver impromptu questions on any subject they wished to those students wishing to demonstrate exceptional knowledge or ingenuity, although attendance was purely optional. Specialist examinations in mathematics then developed (again, these were originally voluntary), which lasted several days, with candidates standing down when they had demonstrated their full ability, until only one student was left, who would be known as the 'Senior Wrangler'. Other outstanding candidates were listed in order of merit as 'Second', 'Third' or 'Fourth' Wranglers, and so on; students taking first-class degrees in mathematics are still called Wranglers.

Other mathematics graduates were classed as Senior and Junior Optimes (from the Latin 'optime disputati', 'you have argued very well'). The lowest-ranking Junior Optime was presented with a wooden spoon by his fellow students. This developed into an elaborate painted object, 5ft long, which was lowered from The Senate House balcony at the graduation ceremony, bearing a Greek inscription which can be translated as:

> In honours mathematical
> This is the very last of all:
> The Wooden Spoon which you see here
> O you who see it, shed a tear.

DEGREE DAY   PRESENTATION OF THE WOODEN SPOON

The wooden spoon being lowered from the Senate House gallery at the graduation ceremony.
(*Author's collection*)

Cambridge University is unique in referring to degree examinations as the 'Tripos'. Disputations were held before a senior member of the university, who was known as Mr Tripos or 'The Bachelor of the Stool', as he sat on a three-legged chair and made speeches for the occasion, called 'Tripos Verses'. These were published with a list of successful mathematics graduates in order of accomplishment – the 'Tripos List' – with the result that mathematics examinations came to be called the Tripos. Examinations in Classics (Latin and Greek), known as the 'Classics Tripos', were introduced in 1824: Hensleigh Wedgewood (who later became a leading lawyer and natural historian) received the lowest marks of the year, after which the lowest-ranking classics graduate was called the 'Wedge'. Printed examination papers on subjects directly related to students' courses of study began to be published in 1827. Disputations were abolished in 1839 (by which time they were often little more than standard questions and replies). Students at King's College were automatically awarded degrees on leaving Cambridge until 1851, when the decision by the Fellows of the college that the students would have to take an examination marked the initiation of the present examination system. The term 'tripos examinations' has since expanded to include all Cambridge University examinations, even in such obviously modern subjects as computer studies.

Cambridge MAs form a body collectively known as the Senate (after the ruling assembly of the Roman Empire). The Senate discussed university business in meetings known as congregations, held in Great St Mary's Church until 1738, and the Senate House thereafter. Formal motions were called graces. All members of the Senate could attend a congregation and discuss graces, which were passed or rejected by majority vote. By the fourteenth century it became practical to refer most matters to a representative body known as the Caput Senatus, anglicised as the Council of the Senate, then abbreviated to the Council, now comprising nineteen members, which remains the university's executive body.

The Chancellor is the theoretical head of the university. The Chancellorship is the oldest post in the university, documented from 1228. The Chancellor originally oversaw the

The Chancellor heading a university procession. (*Cambridgeshire Collection, Cambridge Central Library*)

running of the university, but from the fifteenth century the office was conferred on prominent national figures in the hope they might advance university interests. Appointed for life, he appears at important ceremonies, and often takes a great interest in the university, but no longer plays a direct role in university affairs.

From the late thirteenth century a Vice-Chancellor began to deputise for the Chancellor, and took over the Chancellor's duties as that post became distanced from university life. The Vice-Chancellor is now chosen from leading university academics to be the university's first officer and head of the Council. Formerly the appointment was for two years, but since 1990 it has been for seven years. Modern British universities copy this system, appointing a national figure as an honorary Chancellor while choosing a Vice-Chancellor from the academic staff.

Two Proctors (a name derived from the ancient Roman office of procurator) are the leading University officials after the Vice-Chancellor. They organise timetables, supervise official functions and maintain University discipline. Documented from the thirteenth century, they are appointed from the College Fellows on a complicated rotational system called the Proctorial Cycle. Upon appointment the Senior Proctor receives two staffs, while the Junior Proctor receives a staff and a metal tube known as a 'Butter Measure' (in fact a corn gauge for sampling grain), symbolising the authority Proctors once held to regulate weights and measures in Cambridge. At one time the Proctors could apprehend any woman suspected of prostitution within Cambridge and commit her to a short spell of detention in a private university prison, attached to the local workhouse, called the Spinning House. This practice was abolished in 1894 after two women, Jane Elsden and Daisy Hopkins, apprehended while walking through Cambridge, sued the university for wrongful arrest.

The Proctors' authority was upheld by two constables, or 'Bulldogs', who wore black suits and bowler hats. Bulldogs could apprehend any student found breaking regulations, take their details and report them to the Proctors for appropriate action. Recalcitrant students who spotted the Bulldogs often tried to run from them, and it was traditionally said that one Bulldog was selected as a sprinter, to apprehend students attempting a quick getaway, while the other was chosen for endurance, to chase those capable of prolonged flight.

Until 1973 Proctors maintained a nightwatch, when they might enter pubs, cinemas and places of public entertainment to check student behaviour, and they still investigate and punish students accused of breaking university regulations.

The university still appoints between twenty and thirty constables, who help to maintain order and security at university functions. Although they do not actively enforce the law, they do assist the local police force when necessary.

Proctors are assisted by Pro-Proctors, including a Motor Proctor who regulates undergraduate ownership of motor cars. Car ownership and allocation of permanent parking places is restricted, as it would cause great congestion if every student owned a car. The relatively flat geography of Cambridge means that nearly every student acquires a bicycle on arrival at the university, and cycles between academic, social and business commitments. Cycle ownership has spread throughout the city, and, although it is impossible to estimate the number, there must surely be little doubt that there are more bicycles per capita in regular use in Cambridge than in any other town or city in the United Kingdom.

Perhaps the students thought that being with their bicycles they did not have to wear their gowns.
(*Cambridgeshire Collection, Cambridge Central Library*)

Since 1521 an Orator has been appointed to compose and read Latin speeches on ceremonial occasions. The poet George Herbert called the post 'the finest place in the university'. Recent attempts to end the use of Latin have been resoundingly defeated.

Two Esquire Bedells, a name derived from the term 'beadle', served as intermediaries between the town and the university and acted as messengers. Documented since 1250, they were once appointed for life to act as unofficial guardians of university protocol and procedure. Like the Chancellorship, these appointments are now largely ceremonial.

Some defunct offices were intriguing. Taxors 'taxed' or assessed rents between 1231 and 1855. Until 1858 a Yeoman, Inferior or Dog Bedell publicly announced university events and delivered court summonses. The Master of Glomery ran the medieval grammar school and awarded degrees in grammar (a subject which then included the study of Latin and self-expression). His authority was upheld by a Bedell in Glomery. On graduating, a Master of Grammar (known as a Glomeral) was presented with a rod, symbolising authority to teach and maintain discipline. A young boy was brought forward, and publicly beaten by the new Master; the boy received a groat (fourpenny coin) as a reward. The Master of Glomery disappeared from the university records after 1539, probably to the relief of the town's youth.

In 1604 Cambridge University became a parliamentary constituency, returning two MPs until 1911 and one thereafter until 1950, when the seat was abolished. Cambridge MAs were thus allowed two votes at elections: for the constituency where they lived, and also for the university. Isaac Newton and William Pitt the Younger were both university MPs.

Academic robes have a language of their own. In the Middle Ages any man with a claim to scholarship might wear a sleeveless gown known as a 'Curtain', and a round, close-fitting cap, and for a long time these continued to be standard university dress. Fellow Commoners wore black robes and tall hats (or purple gowns trimmed with gold lace on special days); Pensioners wore velvet-faced gowns; Sizars wore plain black. Senior university members wore a mortar board, a skullcap topped by a square board, as a privilege, but students were allowed to wear this from 1769. Corpus Christi college introduced an individual college gown in 1828; Clare followed eight years later. All colleges then adopted distinctive gowns, usually black with striped sleeves, although Trinity and Gonville and Caius students wear dark blue.

Students had to wear robes in public and when attending academic activities on pain of a 6s 8d fine: Proctors and Bulldogs regularly patrolled Cambridge to maintain costume regulations. Some exemptions came to be permitted, as gowns were a hindrance in laboratory experiments and dangerous when riding a bicycle. Mortar boards passed from use during the Second World War owing to shortages of material, but the obligation to wear gowns was not abolished until 1965 when costume regulations came to be seen as impractical and unenforceable, since the number of students and townspeople had grown

Theodore Roosevelt, who had served two terms as President of the USA, received an honorary Cambridge degree in 1910. He stands in the centre in ceremonial robes with the Esquire Bedells, Arthur Humble Evans and Alfred Page Humphrey on the left and Canon Arthur James Mason of Pembroke College, the Vice-Chancellor, and Alfred Brocket Sheldrick, the University Marshal (in top hat), on the right.
(Cambridgeshire Collection, Cambridge Central Library)

Corpus Christi students in graduation gowns with the Master of the College.
(*Cambridgeshire Collection, Cambridge Central Library*)

'Your name and college, sir!' A Proctor and Bulldog stop two young men on suspicion of being students
who have broken costume regulations by venturing into Cambridge without gowns.
This was probably posed for the camera. (*Cambridgeshire Collection, Cambridge Central Library*)

so greatly that it became impossible to distinguish who was a student. The consensus of opinion, even among the most conservative dons, was that these rules were too archaic, even for Cambridge!

University members are still expected to wear gowns at official events such as graduation ceremonies or royal visits, known as Scarlet Days, since Doctors of Divinity, Law or Medicine wear scarlet gowns, while Doctors of Philosophy wear black gowns with scarlet facings. Attendant staff who control visitor admissions at King's College wear gowns when on duty; the college's tourist liaison officer informs me that these are a surprising symbol of authority, and the appearance of a monitor in a gown is normally sufficient to disarm disruptive or disagreeable visitors!

Cambridge University was slow to admit women. Emily Davies and Anne Jemima Clough opened the colleges of Girton and Newnham in 1873 and 1875 respectively: there women could sit examinations, though they could not yet take degrees, even after Agnata Frances Ramsey and Philippa Fawcett (daughter of Henry Fawcett, see page 9) had achieved the highest marks of the year in the classics and mathematics tripos. In 1887, and again in 1897, congregations rejected graces that women should take degrees. On the second occasion anti-female feeling reached such a height that male undergraduates burnt an effigy of a female student on Market Hill, defaced the gates of Girton College, and mobbed the

William Chaffy, Master of Sidney Sussex College, and Vice-Chancellor in 1813 and 1829, in Scarlet Day robes. (*Cambridgeshire Collection, Cambridge Central Library*)

Proctors and Bulldogs when they tried to restore order. In 1920, the last time a congregation was convened to take a free vote, women were permitted to take degrees by a majority of 1,011 to 369, but denied full university membership by 908 votes to 694. Women were finally allowed full membership of the university in 1948. Colleges later became co-educational; in 1987, Magdalen College became the last men's college to admit women. Rosemary Murray, the first female Vice-Chancellor, took office in 1975.

Early in the twentieth century the expression 'rag' came to mean organised student fooling. This became synonymous with Rag Day from 1921, when students organised the town's Poppy Day collection for disabled ex-servicemen on the Saturday nearest to 11 November (Armistice Day). Poppy Day Rags became an occasion for festivity as students engaged in increasingly eccentric fund-raising activities, which included a parade of

Senate House Hill during the 1897 debate on admission of women to degrees.
A congregation was called to vote on the subject: the number of people present and the banners on
display, show the strong feelings this issue raised at the time.
(*Cambridgeshire Collection, Cambridge Central Library*)

Float at the 1928 Poppy Day Rag on a Dale's Brewery van. (*Cambridgeshire Collection, Cambridge Central Library*)

Float on Market Hill at the 1961 Poppy Day Rag. *(Cambridgeshire Collection, Cambridge Central Library)*

decorated floats and weirdly dressed undergraduates collecting money from spectators or passers-by. After 1966 Rag Day was moved to February and the money raised was divided among several charities. The University Rag has since expanded to encompass a series of fund-raising events lasting throughout the year to raise money for numerous local and national charities. The traditional parade now takes place in March, and this is supplemented by a series of auctions, bazaars and sponsored events. There is also a sponsored jailbreak in which students have thirty-six hours to get as far from Cambridge as possible without spending any money; in 2005 two reached Hong Kong. In 2006 Cambridge University Rag raised over £160,000 for 100 charities. Each year there are efforts to outperform previous rags, and if any reader wishes to make a donation, however small, to the latest rag, I know it will be greatly appreciated.

3 ALL CREATURES GREAT AND SMALL

One of the strangest events in the history of Cambridge must be the discovery of a fish that had swallowed a book. On 23 June 1626 a fishmonger on Peas Hill cut open a cod, delivered from King's Lynn an hour previously, to find a canvas bundle in its stomach. This attracted a crowd of people, including Dr Joseph Mead from Christ's College, who described the event in a letter (contained in the British Library's *Harley Manuscripts*) to his friend, Sir Martin Stuteville of Dalham in Suffolk. Taking command of the situation, Dr Mead split the canvas with his knife to find a book. Although partly decomposed and smelling horribly, much of the print was still legible. 'I saw with mine own eyes the fish, the maw, the piece of sail cloth, the book, and observed all I have written,' he wrote. 'He that had his nose as near as I did yester morning would have been persuaded that there was no imposture there without witness.' The book was taken to the Vice-Chancellor of the university, and was found to contain three Christian tracts. One was by John Frith, an early Protestant thinker, written, by an amazing coincidence, while the

A fish stall on Peas Hill, the Cambridge fish market. (*Cambridgeshire Collection, Cambridge Central Library*)

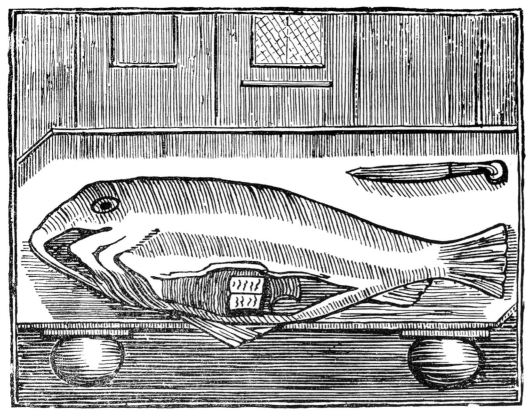

The frontispiece of *Vox Pisces*, showing the book's discovery in the fish's stomach.
(From the *East Anglian* magazine)

author was imprisoned in a fish cellar. They were published with the title *Vox Pisces: Or The Book Fish Containing Three Treatises Which Were Found In The Belly Of A Cod Fish*. Many people said it was a divine message, although nobody was quite sure what this might be. Cod are known for voracious appetites: they swim with their mouths open, swallowing anything that passes in, though it has never been satisfactorily explained how one swallowed a book!

Some colleges do not allow students to keep pets, and the history of Trinity College shows an ambivalent attitude to dogs. When James I stayed there in 1613 several eminent dons held a debate to decide whether dogs could make syllogisms (logical conclusions from deductive reasoning). When the dons concluded that dogs could not think James challenged them, saying his dogs were an exception, which was greeted with cheers from the audience.

In 1665 a college official was given an extra duty of keeping dogs out of the college chapel, and by the eighteenth century college rules forbade even Fellows from keeping dogs. This was not lost on the poet George, Lord Byron, who was admitted to Trinity in 1805 when aged 17, as a Fellow Commoner, a privileged position given to sons of wealthy families. An animal lover, Lord Byron was devoted to his dogs, and adopted a largely vegetarian diet. When he acquired a bulldog, Smut, he was informed that he could not keep it at college. Observing that there was no rule to prevent him from keeping a pet bear, he bought a bear. He wrote to his sister Elizabeth, 'I have got a new friend, the finest in the world, a tame bear. When I brought him here they asked me what I meant to do with him, and my reply was he should sit for a Fellowship.' Byron's close friend Ned Long wrote, 'I make no doubt Bruin [the bear] would receive a Fellow of Trinity with a friendly hug.' The bear was probably a performing animal that had been trained to dance (possibly by very brutal means). Lord Byron may have bought it from its keeper, perhaps at Sturbridge Fair, when such 'entertainments' frequented Cambridge.

Some college histories say Lord Byron kept the bear in one of the octagonal turrets in the corners of the Great Court. This is unlikely; he was more likely to have used the stables of the Ram Inn where Trinity students stabled their horses. (Long demolished, this stood in Round Church Street.)

On leaving Trinity Byron took the bear to his family seat at Newstead in Nottinghamshire, where it died in 1810. It is plausible that he was not simply flouting college rules by keeping a bear. Thomas Clarkson and William Wilberforce had just persuaded Parliament to abolish the slave trade, and Byron may have been arguing against the exploitation of animals. Byron was unimpressed by university life: as a Fellow Commoner he made no effort to study, yet knew he would automatically receive a degree. Richard Porson, the Master of Trinity, was a notorious alcoholic who physically attacked students (and other dons) when drunk. Byron may have been jibing at college regulations that prohibited pets but ignored poor academic standards, suggesting university values were so low that a performing bear could become a don.

The Gogmagog Hills were home to the Godolphin Arabian, who occupies an important place in the history of British horseracing. Born in the Yemen in 1724, he was originally known as Sham (the Arabic name for Damascus) and was one of a group of Arabian horses that the Bey of Tunis presented to Louis XV of France when they made a trade agreement.

Edward Coke, a Derbyshire landowner and a leading figure in the contemporary sporting world, visited the French court, where he bought Sham. On his death in 1733 Edward Coke left his horses to his agent, Roger Williams, and his friend, Francis, the second Earl Godolphin. Lord Godolphin bought Sham from Roger Williams and took the horse to his country seat at Wandlebury on the Gogmagog Hills, where he became known as the Godolphin Arabian.

Although he was never raced competitively, the Godolphin Arabian was an excellent stud stallion, lending powers of speed to his offspring. He sired a string

The Godolphin Arabian.
(*Cambridgeshire Collection, Cambridge Central Library*)

The Godolphin Arabian's grave in the eighteenth-century stable block at Wandlebury, a focus of pilgrimage for horse-racing enthusiasts. (*Author's collection*)

of champions, including Lath and Regulus, the best racehorses of the day. All British racehorses, and many others in the English-speaking world, trace their ancestry to either the Darley Arabian, the Byerley Turk or the Godolphin Arabian. When he died in 1753 (supposedly on Christmas Day), aged 29, the Godolphins held a wake in his honour, with cakes and ale. He was buried in the stable block at Wandlebury, where his grave remains a focus of pilgrimage for racing enthusiasts the world over. He has been the subject of a biographical romance by the French author Eugene Sue and Margaret Henry's children's novel *King of the Wind* (adapted as a film in 1989, with a cast including Jenny Agutter, Frank Finlay, Richard Harris, Nigel Hawthorne and Glenda Jackson).

At the north-east corner of the garden enclosure at Wandlebury there are ten small headstones to pets of the Gray family (who lived there from 1904 to 1953) and others from the estate. Most only give names, but three are dated to 1918, 1924 and 1938. An eleventh stone to Heidi, dated 1988, evidently placed by a modern resident, completes the line-up.

The Wandlebury pet cemetery. (*Author's collection*)

The Godolphin Arabian's career can be compared with that of Jimmy, a donkey who became well known in Peterborough. The German and Allied armies both used horses, donkeys and mules for transport during the First World War. At the Battle of the Somme some soldiers from the Scottish Rifles (popularly known as the Cameronians) captured a German emplacement, where they found a dead female donkey who had recently given birth. They took the colt back to their own emplacements, called him Jimmy, reared him and treated him as a mascot – making him one of the few participants in the First World War to change sides without attracting animosity.

At the end of the war when most of the soldiers were demobilised, many of the animals used by the military were sold off. Jimmy was sent to a military depot at Swaythling, near Southampton, and bought by Mr Walding, a Peterborough tradesman. On arrival at Peterborough Mrs Heath, the secretary of the local branch of the RSPCA, was so touched by his story that she initiated a subscription to buy him by showing him at the town's Hippodrome. Money poured in, allowing her to buy Jimmy, who then raised funds for the RSPCA and appeared at charity events. When not fund-raising he grazed on Burghley Square. After he died in 1943 he was buried in Peterborough's Central Park under a memorial to 'Our Jimmy'. This later fell into decay, but was restored in 2002, and unveiled in a ceremony at which the Peterborough branches of the British Legion and Army Cadet Corps laid wreaths.

The county's lost attractions include the pet cemetery at Molesworth. Opened in 1904, by a Mr Gray, whose brother kept the dogs' cemetery in London's Hyde Park, within five years 130 pets had been buried there: mostly dogs, but also thirty cats, ten birds and one monkey. In 1917 a titled lady from Portland Square was fined £50 for wasting petrol during the wartime emergency after hiring a taxi to take her dog there for burial.

Pets' (mostly dogs') graves at Molesworth Pet Cemetery, now lost. (*Author's collection*)

Once a popular visitor attraction, the cemetery fell out of use at about the time of the Second World War, and most of the memorials have been removed or destroyed. Only a few remain at the end of the garden of a private house, inaccessible to the public. In 2006 the present owner showed me the remaining memorials, mostly rather neglected and overgrown, the most moving of which was a little statue of a dog on a column, with the inscription 'In loving memory of Bibby who went to Dreamland 10 March 1910. Affectionate, honest and true.'

An often overlooked pet memorial stands at Mitcham's Corner in Cambridge, at the apex of an island site where Chesterton Road and Victoria Road diverge, in front of the Lloyds TSB Bank. An 18in-high stone bears the inscription: '1934 IN MEMORY OF TONY A DOG WHO GAVE HIM FRIENDSHIP AND HAPPINESS DURING HIS CAMBRIDGE YEARS THIS TROUGH IS ERECTED BY HIS ROYAL HIGHNESS PRINCE CHULA OF SIAM'.

Prince Chula Chakrabongse, a grandson of Rama V of Thailand (formerly Siam), studied at Trinity College from 1930 to 1934. As Thailand became a republic in 1932 Prince Chula and his cousin, Prince Bira, stayed in England, becoming leading figures in the motor-racing world. As the inscription shows, Chula's dog died during his final year at Cambridge. The memorial was a dog's drinking fountain, connected to Cambridge's mains water supply. Apparently the tap was still working in 1964, though it has long since been cut off. Facing outwards from the road junction, where hedges have been planted in front of it, it is not easily noticed unless one stands on the front steps of the Lloyds TSB Bank.

A cats' cemetery in the garden of Peckover House, the National Trust showplace in Wisbech, includes seven headstones and three fragmentary memorials, some dated between 1883 and 1935. Although rather worn, legible inscriptions to what were evidently pets of the Peckover family include 'Marmie, my most beautiful and loving orange cat' and 'Angel, loving and faithful'.

Elsie Bambridge, the last private owner of Wimpole Hall – she left it to the National Trust in 1976 – created a small burial ground for her dogs just outside the fence of the church-yard which adjoins the hall. Three small headstones commemorate Issy,

Memorial to Marmie in the Peckover House cats' cemetery. (*Author's collection*)

Memorials to Issy, Primo and Jess, between the hall and the parish churchyard at Wimpole.
(*Author's collection*)

Primo and Jess, buried between 1939 and 1973. The inscriptions say that Issy was born in Brussels, while Primo originated from Madrid.

Colonel T. Walter Harding, a Yorkshire industrialist who bought Madingley Hall in 1905, also desired to commemorate his Jack Russell terriers. The central feature of the topiary garden at Madingley Hall is an armillary sphere on a column: close inspection reveals the inscription 'MY BELOVED NANKI 1903–1919 *Colligor ex ipso dominae placuisse sepulchro*'. This is a quote from the sixth elegy in Ovid's *Amores*, which can be freely translated as 'From this memorial you may see what love my mistress bore to me.'

Colonel Harding later set up a pet cemetery in a wooded area just outside the south-west perimeter of the gardens. Six small memorials, all now badly damaged and worn, mark the resting place of other Jack Russell terriers. These too bear short Latin inscriptions; some are now illegible, but one, to Ming, reads '*Amicus fidelis, vale!*' or 'Farewell, faithful friend!' (This wood is now private property with no public access.)

Rare wild birds and animals have been found in Cambridgeshire, although it is a sad fact that some of the most unusual have been driven to extinction. The great bustard was common until the eighteenth century. The largest European wild bird, a typical male can be 45in high with a 4ft wingspan and weigh 40lb, while a female can be 36in high with a 38in wingspan and weigh 26lb. Ground-nesting birds, they prefer to live in open countryside. They were once common on Royston and Newmarket Heaths: there was a field called Bustard Leys at Melbourn, and there is also a road at Kimbolton called Bustard

Hill. There are records from the seventeenth century of their being shot for food, and even hunted with greyhounds near Newmarket.

Yet the great bustard's extinction in Cambridgeshire was not due to hunting or food consumption but the Agricultural Revolution. The expansion of agriculture during the Napoleonic Wars, combined with the enclosure of open fields, destroyed its natural habitat, and between 1800 and 1830 the British population fell exponentially. There are occasional records of sightings in subsequent decades — a pair spent several weeks on Burwell Fen in 1856 — but they had vanished from Cambridgeshire by the end of the century. They are commemorated as supporters on the county coat of arms.

Whittlesey Mere was the largest lake in England outside the Lake District. Covering 1,600 acres (2½ square miles), it was drained between 1849 and 1853. The Large Copper Butterfly (*Lycaena dispar*), the largest of its species, was unique to the mere and the adjoining

In 1976 J.P. Brooke-Little, Richmond Herald, designed a coat of arms for the new administrative county of Cambridgeshire incorporating two great bustards as supporters. (*Author's collection*)

marshes. It died out in the 1840s, even before the lake was drained, possibly owing to the regular burning of mereside reed beds. Since the 1920s a related species (*Lycaena dispar batavus*) has been bred at Woodwalton Fen.

A subspecies of the edible or water frog (*Rana esculenta*) was once common in parts of Cambridgeshire. Its largest breeding grounds were the Great Moor, the lake from which Fowlmere derived its name, where the particularly loud croak of these frogs led to their being called Dutch Nightingales or Whaddon Angels (as they also bred at nearby Whaddon). They attracted the attention of the British zoological community in 1843, when a natural historian from Duxford sent two to the British Museum. The following year more were sent to the University Museum of Zoology at Cambridge.

The French edible frog had been introduced to the British Isles in 1837, and it was suggested that the Fowlmere frogs could have been French imports that migrated (or perhaps hopped) rather rapidly into Cambridgeshire. However, investigation showed this was not the case, for while the better-known French specimens belong to the variant *typica*, Fowlmere Frogs belonged to the less common *lesonae* variant, a subspecies which had previously only been known in Northern Italy. There was some debate as to how they could have spread so far north. The monks of Vercelli Abbey in Lombardy were Lords of the Manor of Chesterton, and maintained a manor house there, so it was suggested that the monks imported them to Chesterton, from where they went native. People have always transported breeding animals for food potential (the rabbit was introduced to Britain by the Normans and then by the British to Australia and North America), but the idea of Italian

The Great Moor at Fowlmere, once the breeding grounds for the edible frog (*Rana esculenta*) now a nature reserve. (*Author's collection*)

monks transporting frogs over the Alps to Cambridgeshire does sound rather far-fetched. In the following years colonies were found elsewhere in Northern Europe, suggesting that dispersal occurred naturally.

However, the drainage of the Great Moor in 1845 caused this frog to vanish from the Fowlmere area, although naturalists have occasionally found other specimens elsewhere in the Fens or on the Fen Edge. There is no indication that these (or any other) frogs were eaten in Cambridgeshire in recent times.

Some supernatural animals have also appeared in the county. A thirteenth-century legend says that a phantom knight haunts the Wandlebury Ring on the Gogmagog Hills. If challenged to combat at midnight he will charge on horseback. A warrior called Osbert Fitzhugh challenged and defeated him, and took his horse back to Cambridge, but it burst from its stables at midnight and disappeared. Abbey House, a seventeenth-century mansion near the Newmarket Road in Cambridge, is said to be haunted by several ghosts, including a little animal running on its hind legs that is only seen by children.

For nearly thirty years there have been many sightings of a large black cat across Cambridgeshire. Despite its black colour, it was inevitably called the Fen Tiger (a long-established nickname for a native Fenlander). The *Cambridge Evening News* has reported sightings: one early appearance was at Bourn Airfield in 1978. One of the better seasons for appearances was 1994. Dan Ashman, a Welsh zoology student, observed it in Whittlesford one morning; when he approached the creature it crouched low and hissed, causing him to withdraw, but he collected some of its droppings. Dan estimated it to have been 4ft 6in long and 2ft 6in high; a local pensioner also said he had previously seen the beast. Jill Unwin of Impington, woken by a noise at 2 a.m., saw a cat 'as big as a Labrador' jump over her garden fence. Deborah Roberts, a Fowlmere parish councillor, saw it twice in her garden. William Rooker was filming local aircraft at Cottenham with a video camera when a large black animal appeared. William filmed the creature for two minutes: it slinked across the field, then sat down, before darting away at some speed. As it stayed 150yds away precise identification was difficult. One zoologist said it resembled a cat, but might have been a puma or leopard. Few sightings are quite so dramatic, but the *Cambridge Evening News* records that thirty-four big-cat sightings were reported between January 2003 and March 2004. It has been suggested that one or more wild cats might have been kept at zoos or wildlife parks, or as exotic pets, and escaped from captivity, or even have been released by an irresponsible owner. Yet domesticated and even semi-domesticated animals will not greatly avoid humans, while the Fen Tiger persistently shuns people.

The Fen Tiger could be considered Cambridgeshire's equivalent of the Loch Ness Monster, and the debate over its existence has followed similar lines. Most people might concede that there have been so many sightings that they cannot all be dismissed as fraud or overactive imagination, and some zoologists are ready to give serious consideration to at least some witness testimony. There have been sufficient reports for enough years to suggest the existence of several beasts, even a breeding population. Sceptics argue that wild cats would eat other animals, and each kill should leave distinct traces, yet these are seldom seen. It has also been questioned why no dead wild cat has been found; or why there has been no incontrovertible sighting by many people at close range. But while the Loch Ness Monster is confined to a single (admittedly large) lake, the Fen Tiger roams a vast swathe of countryside. As with the Loch Ness Monster, if just one of these creatures was to be captured

The Loch Ness Monster was sighted in Cambridge in 1953, when he altruistically helped to raise money for charity. Because the photograph was taken during the university rag week some hardened sceptics argued that this was not really the Loch Ness Monster, but a rag-week float. The author must leave the readers to judge the photograph's authenticity for themselves.
(*Cambridgeshire Collection, Cambridge Central Library*)

it could overturn many preconceptions about zoology, but these animals remain remarkably elusive. It might also be argued that a world without mystery would be a much duller place.

A sign at Madingley warns of toads crossing. (*Author's collection*)

Madingley Toad Rescue started in 1988. Lakes in the grounds of Madingley Hall are breeding grounds for local toads. To reach the lakes many cross the roads, where they get run over, particularly since their peak migration corresponds with the local rush hour. Thus a 'toad tunnel' has been built under the village street to permit amphibians to cross in safety. Between mid-February (many animals begin the mating season at about Valentine's Day) and the spring low polythene fences are placed along the roadsides to prevent toads straying onto the roads, and nets are placed over drains. In the evening there are toad searches, the purpose of which is to carry the waiting toads across the road in safety; over 1,000 are saved in this manner every year. Madingley Toad Rescue shows how individuals, even without large resources or funding, can make a positive difference to wildlife conservation.

4 ARCHITECTURAL CURIOSITIES

Cambridgeshire possesses a wide and varied architectural heritage, and many buildings in the county tell fascinating stories. One such place is Hemingford Grey Manor House, the oldest continually inhabited family house in Britain. It was built in about 1140, probably for Payn de Hemingford, the Norman Lord of the Manor. Over the centuries new ceilings and a solid central chimney stack were added, then in the eighteenth century a large house was built around it. Much of this was destroyed by a fire at the end of the eighteenth century, but Payn de Hemingford's stone house survived comparatively unscathed. The walls (apart from the north wall, which is a survival of the eighteenth-century mansion) are of Barnack stone, 3ft thick.

Exterior view of Hemingford Grey Manor House. Although the north front (to the left) was erected in the eighteenth century, the west-facing round-headed window to the right is twelfth century. (*Diana Boston*)

In 1937 Lucy Boston bought Hemingford Grey, and began a conscientious, painstaking and sensitive restoration, highlighting its historic features, yet maintaining it as a dwelling where she could live with her family; she went on to plant a beautiful garden around the house. During the Second World War she provided twice-weekly gramophone-record recitals for members of the RAF stationed locally. From 1954 Lucy's dedication to the house inspired her to write eleven novels about its history, including the *Green Knowe* series, six time fantasies set in the house, the fourth of which, *A Stranger At Green Knowe*, was awarded the Carnegie Medal for the outstanding children's book of 1961. Lucy Boston wrote these as novels and they are only regarded as children's books because her publishers marketed them as such. Communicating important messages about the connections between the past and present and the environment and conservation, like many works classified as children's books they exhibit genuine literary power and should be read by all ages.

Hemingford Grey Manor is now owned by Lucy's daughter-in-law, Diana Boston, who organises tours of the house by appointment. These can be booked in advance, and are memorable occasions, when the history of the house and Lucy Boston's experiences there are described vividly.

School of Pythagoras

The School of Pythagoras, in the grounds of St John's College, Cambridge, is the county's second-oldest house. It was built in the later twelfth century for the Dunning family, who were among the town's wealthiest families; Hervey Dunning became the first mayor of Cambridge in 1207. At that time a house built in stone was so unusual that it was simply

School of Pythagoras in 1908. (*Cambridgeshire Collection, Cambridge Central Library*)

known as the Stone House. Hervey Dunning's son Eustace fell into debt and sold the house and surrounding land to Walter de Merton, who presented it to Merton College at Oxford University, which he had just founded. Oxford and Cambridge Universities were originally insecure and unstable organisations – as previously stated, Cambridge University was established when students fled Oxford in a dispute with the town authorities – and Walter probably acquired the house in case the students were obliged to leave Oxford again.

By 1574 the building was known as the School of Pythagoras. Even then it would have been recognised as one of Cambridge's oldest houses, so it might have been pointed out as the first home of the university. At that time Oxford and Cambridge Universities were busy devising highly fanciful stories to prove that each was the older and historically more important. It was claimed that Cambridge University was founded by one of the great Greek philosophers, and Pythagoras may have been forwarded as a candidate. Yet the school hardly received the respect one might expect for the academy of a classical philosopher: pigs may have been kept there until in 1502 when a lease forbade it. In the sixteenth century it became an annexe and storeroom for a larger house to the north. Fortunately, by the nineteenth century its historical importance was being appreciated, which led to its preservation. St John's College bought it in 1958, and it is now a theatre for student productions.

Denny Abbey

A farmhouse standing in isolation in the fields near Waterbeach contains the remains of Denny Abbey, a medieval monastery. Founded in 1159 as a cell of Ely Cathedral, in 1170,

Denny Abbey was converted into a farmhouse after the Dissolution. Medieval structural features can still be discerned. (*Cambridgeshire Collection, Cambridge Central Library*)

when only half-complete, it was transferred to the Knights Templar. Denny Abbey became a hospital for sick members of the order, as well as a commandery or religious and military outpost.

In 1308 the Knights Templars were dissolved by Philip IV of France, largely to obtain their funds. Many English Templars joined the Knights Hospitallers, and Denny, like several Templar houses, was transferred to the Hospitallers. Then, in 1327, Edward III presented Denny to Mary de Valence, Countess of Pembroke, who moved a community of Franciscan nuns (also known as Poor Clares) there. The Countess used half the building as a personal apartment, and the nuns lived and worshipped in the other half, while a new church was built to the east. Thirty-five nuns still lived there when it was dissolved in 1538. To the end, the nuns maintained a spirit of religious devotion: when the abbey was dissolved the last abbess, Elizabeth Throckmorton, retired to her family home Coughton Court in Warwickshire, where she and other nuns continued to live in obedience to their vows until their deaths.

Denny was the only medieval English monastery to be used by four different monastic orders of both monks and nuns, and is one of the best-preserved Templar houses in England. Although the nuns' church was demolished, large sections of the other buildings were turned into a farmhouse, since when historians and archaeologists have had great fun trying to work out which part of the abbey was built by which monastic order. Now regularly open to the public, its grounds house the Farmland Museum.

Longthorpe Manor House

Longthorpe Manor House is believed to have been built in the 1260s by Sir William Thorpe, who had Longthorpe Church rebuilt at the same time. William's son, Robert Thorpe, added a three-storey tower, about 40ft high, to the house during the early fourteenth century. The manor house became a farmhouse and the tower was used as a lookout by the Home Guard during the Second World War. In 1946 Hugh Horrell, the

Longthorpe Tower.
(Author's collection)

owner, decided to turn the upper chamber into a bedroom. Scraping plaster off the walls, he found a series of medieval wall paintings. The paintings date from the second quarter of the fourteenth century and include coats of arms, Fenland birds, a wheel of the five senses – showing a monkey eating (taste), a spider in its web (touch), a boar with pricked ears (hearing), a vulture (smell) and a cock (sight) with 'reason' in the centre – and a cycle showing the seven ages of man. Over the door there is a boncannon, a mythical creature which defended itself by excreting on its pursuer, possibly a warning to unwanted guests. These form the most complete set of medieval domestic wall paintings in England. In the Middle Ages the room must have glowed like an illuminated manuscript. Visits to Longthorpe Tower can be made, but should be booked in advance.

Gatehouses

Some gatehouses have been moved to new sites. Sections of Ramsey Abbey gatehouse, for example, were moved to Hinchingbrooke Hall, near Huntingdon. At the Dissolution of the Monasteries much monastic property in Huntingdonshire was granted to Sir Richard Cromwell, a nephew and favourite relative of Thomas Cromwell (Henry VIII's chief minister and architect of the Dissolution). Richard's son, Sir Henry Cromwell, rebuilt a former nunnery at Hinchingbrooke as a second residence, having the front section of Ramsey Abbey gatehouse transported there to provide a spectacular entrance to the park. Two ferocious 'wild men' with clubs stand guard on either side of the entrance. Wild men often appear at entrances to medieval buildings: did they symbolise guardian spirits, or signify the change from a hostile outside world to a civilised home?

Sir Henry (whose second son, Robert, was the father of Oliver Cromwell) was known as the Golden Knight for his opulent lifestyle and conspicuous expenditure. This was exemplified by his building programme, which depleted the family fortunes to such an extent that the Cromwells sold Hinchingbrooke to the Montague family in 1627.

Edward II founded King's Hall College at Cambridge in 1317. This stood on King's Childer Lane, which ran from the modern Trinity Street to the Cam. King Edward's

The gatehouse to the Cromwell family's mansion at Hinchingbrooke, transported stone by stone from Ramsey Abbey. (*Author's collection*)

King Edward's Tower at Trinity College, Cambridge. (*Author's collection*)

Kirtling Tower: this sixteenth-century gatehouse was spared when Kirtling Hall was demolished in 1806. Gatehouses are often preserved after demolition of the rest of the building. (Kirtling Tower is not open to the public.) (*Author's collection*)

Tower, the first college gatehouse at Cambridge, was built between 1428 and 1432. In 1547 Henry VIII merged King's Hall and Michaelhouse Colleges in his own foundation of Trinity College. King's Childer Lane and King's Hall College were then cleared away to make space for Trinity College's Great Court. King Edward's Tower, considered worthy of preservation, was dismantled and moved 90ft north to its present location.

In 1475 Thomas Rotherham financed a gatehouse to the Schools Building at Cambridge. Successively Bishop of Rochester and Lincoln, and Archbishop of York, Thomas Rotherham was Chancellor of the university between 1469 and 1492. His gatehouse was demolished in 1754, whereupon Sir John Hynde Cotton of Madingley Hall bought it for 10 guineas, to be reassembled as a side entrance to Madingley Hall.

Gatehouses can possess symbolic significance, expressing the builder's power and stature, and defining spheres of authority and influence. It is intriguing to see how often they are retained when the rest of a building is demolished or rebuilt: the Cromwell family (perhaps unconsciously) adapted the gatehouse of Ramsey, Huntingdonshire's largest abbey, to demonstrate their new role as lords of the county; the gatehouse of King's Hall college was possibly preserved as a symbol of the continuity of university life and royal patronage, Sir John Cotton conceivably wishing to show himself as an inheritor or guardian of the university tradition. When Cambridge Castle and St Neots Priory were demolished in Tudor times, their gatehouses were preserved until the nineteenth century; Kirtling Hall, the county's largest Tudor mansion, was demolished in 1806, but the gatehouse still stands.

Bridges

Stone bridges over the Ouse at Huntingdon and St Ives show medieval engineering at its best. Construction of Huntingdon Bridge began in 1332. The building of its 215ft span

Huntingdon Bridge. (*Author's collection*)

St Ives Bridge: the eighteenth-century upper storeys of the chapel were demolished in 1928.
(*Author's collection*)

was evidently commenced from both banks, as there is a bend in the middle, presumably marking the junction where the two sides met. It may have been a confident statement of prosperity and importance, as Huntingdon was then one of England's largest and wealthiest towns, with sixteen parish churches. A few years after the bridge's completion Huntingdon was devastated by the Black Death: within a decade three churches had been abandoned and a quarter of the town was deserted. Yet the bridge was so solidly built that it survived, and continues to carry motorised traffic to this day. There was a bridge chapel with a bridge-keeper's house at the town end of the structure: these had been converted into shops by 1572, but have both since disappeared.

A wooden bridge crossing the Ouse was built at St Ives in 1107. This was replaced by the present stone bridge in the fifteenth century, which casts a 200ft span, divided into six arches of different widths. A chapel on a central stone platform in the middle of the river was dedicated to St Leger in 1426, presumably the date of the bridge's completion. A room under the chapel may have been a priest's residence. At the Dissolution Robert Huchyn, the last Prior of St Ives, adapted the chapel as his home. It was later a house, a pub and a doctor's surgery, and in the eighteenth century two extra storeys were added. Tolls were charged for crossing the bridge until 1921; hinge pins from the toll gates can still be seen. During the Civil War parts of both bridges were broken down and replaced by drawbridges in case of Royalist advance. They were rebuilt with round arches in the eighteenth century.

Godmanchester possesses two Chinese-style bridges, reflecting a fashion in English society during the eighteenth and early nineteenth centuries. When Island Hall at Godmanchester was built between 1740 and 1745 its garden included a chinoiserie bridge

The Chinese Bridge at Godmanchester. (*Cambridgeshire Collection, Cambridge Central Library*)

Little Chinese Bridge at Island Hall, Godmanchester. (*Author's collection*)

Watercolour of Clare College Bridge by Marjorie Christine Bates, showing the incomplete parapet ball. (*Author's collection*)

over a tributary of the Ouse. This evidently inspired a similar public footbridge built nearby over the Ouse in 1827 (rebuilt in 1869 and again in 1960). The Island Hall bridge fell into ruin, but was rebuilt by Vane Percy, a new owner, in the 1970s.

Clare College incorporates the oldest and most elegant bridge in Cambridge. Built between 1638 and 1640, the parapet is ornamented by fourteen stone balls. A segment has been cut from the exterior of the south side of one ball. One story relates that a student once carved this away and then bet another student that he either did not know or could not count the number of balls. On being told that there were fourteen, the mischievous first student could show there were in fact 13⅞. Many students are since said to have been duped in the same tedious way.

The Bridge of Sighs at St John's College is the only bridge in the county that is wholly covered and enclosed. Designed in 1831 to link the New Court, west of the Cam, and the older college buildings east of the river, it is named after the similarly covered medieval bridge at Venice, which led to the city prison. There is a small, barred window on the Venetian bridge: it is said that people being led to the prison sighed as they had their last glimpse of freedom through this opening, hence the name. The windows on the bridge in Cambridge are considerably larger, but are similarly barred, supposedly to stop students jumping out on occasions of desperation or high spirits!

The Bridge of Sighs at St John's College, Cambridge. (*Author's collection*)

Theatres

Wisbech's Angles Theatre, one of the country's oldest working theatres, was built in 1793. The actor William Macready performed there in 1836, writing in his diary how he 'acted Hamlet with a load on every limb, sore feet and a mind in a daze'. Closing in 1846, it became a Methodist chapel, a grain store and a tent warehouse, a School of Science and Art, and a Christian Spiritualist Church. In 1978 the Angles Theatre Company was set up with the aim of starting a new theatre in Wisbech, just as the Christian Spiritualist Church was thinking of finding new premises, and the building reverted to its original function. The interior contained remains of a curved front stage (a late eighteenth-century innovation in theatre design) and a gallery extending around three sides of the interior, but so much of these had been lost that the interior had to be wholly rebuilt and remodelled – while an eighteenth-century audience faced north, the audience now faces south. The theatre foyer is of further interest, having been built in 1837 by the Wisbech radical James Hill as the Hall of the People to house a pioneer scheme in public education and co-operative trading.

The Festival Theatre on the Newmarket Road in Cambridge was built in 1814 for the Wilkins family, East Anglian impresarios. It was designed by William Wilkins, a member of the family who became an architect (he later designed the Bury St Edmunds Theatre Royal and London's National Gallery). It was originally called the Barnwell Theatre: at that time the university authorities forbade the staging of plays in Cambridge, so actors performed outside the town limits. Sturbridge Fair was a favoured rendezvous for travelling players, and, though this was in decline by 1814, the theatre was built in the Barnwell area, outside Cambridge and close to the fairground, to attract fair-goers and townspeople (and students who could circumvent university restrictions by attending plays there). In 1878 Robert Sayle bought it to convert into a mission hall for the Evangelisation Society, when it often accommodated more than 500 people (the present permissible maximum is 350). Terence Gray, an entrepreneur and impresario, bought it in 1926, giving it its present name. Independently wealthy, Terence Gray was unconcerned with profits, and he developed it into one of the world's leading avant-garde theatres. Although he rejected scenery and props, Gray replaced the stage with a 'cyclorama', providing what was then Britain's most advanced stage-lighting system. During the Second World War the theatre was run by the Cam Merrymakers, a company who staged productions for off-duty troops. Closing again, it became a warehouse for the Cambridge Arts Theatre. Restoration began in 1990 and proceeded slowly – I saw a play there in 1997, when the building was still in a perilous state, with gaping holes in the roof and walls. But it is now in an immaculate condition, and has been acquired by the Windhorse Trust to become a Buddhist centre.

Estate villages

Chippenham is Britain's earliest estate village, built to a landowner's coherent plan to improve his estate's aesthetics and the lives of his tenants. The manor of Chippenham was acquired in 1696 by Edward Russell, the First Lord of the Admiralty (later Lord Orford), who had a park laid out around his mansion. After 1712, when his park had absorbed half the old village, Russell had a new village built, to include a row of sixteen semi-detached, single-storey cottages, lining the main approach between the park and church, connected by outbuildings, and each fronted by a large garden. A red-brick school was built opposite

Chippenham's eighteenth-century village school (now a private house). (*Author's collection*)

Thorney Village School (now the library and community centre). (*Author's collection*)

the parish church: although now a private house, architecturally it is probably the county's most impressive village school.

Thorney is one of Britain's largest planned Victorian villages. At the Dissolution Thorney Abbey had been granted to the Russell family. Francis Russell, the 4th Duke of Bedford, inherited the family estates in 1839 and initiated an altruistic experiment to turn Thorney into a model community. Like many Victorian landowners the Duke was concerned by stories of drunkenness and crime among his tenants. He believed that the best remedy lay in improved living standards and proper accommodation. Liaising with his estate steward, Tycho Wing, to coordinate the project (many improvements were made at Tycho Wing's suggestion) he commissioned the architect Samuel Saunders Teulon to design new village buildings.

Work took place between 1848 and 1865, when rows of terraced cottages were built, all with gas lighting, a water supply, indoor toilets and a proper waste-disposal system. Each house had a garden, and tenants were also allowed allotments for a small rent. In 1850 a large school for the village children was built opposite the church at a cost of £1,673. Many buildings incorporated Dutch gables, to commemorate the Walloon and French Protestant refugees who had settled here in the seventeenth century. Teulon, being of Huguenot ancestry, was an appropriate choice of architect for the project.

The estate was run from the Tank Yard, an impressive premises built between 1852 and 1855 at a cost of £20,000 to incorporate estate offices, a fire station, a waterworks and a

The Tank Yard, the centre of the Dukes of Bedford's estate at Thorney, incorporating a water tower for an impressive waterworks. A fire service still operates from the building, parts of which have now been adapted as a museum of local history. (*Author's collection*)

sewage-processing plant. Investment in the village paid intangible dividends: during the late nineteenth century Thorney had the county's lowest crime rate and incidence of alcoholism, and the Dukes claimed they never needed to evict a single tenant. The Dukes of Bedford sold their Thorney estate in 1912, but the village retains the largest and most comprehensive display of Victorian cottage architecture in England.

Wimpole Hall's Folly Ruin

Cambridgeshire is not noted for ruins: apart from the Barnack area in the north-west, the county lacks any source of good building stone. Thus, when any church, castle, monastery or mansion ceased to be used its stones were rapidly dismantled for reuse elsewhere.

The county's most impressive ruined castle, in the grounds of Wimpole Hall, is a folly, an ornamental building intended to embellish the landscape. It was designed in 1749 by Sanderson Miller, a Warwickshire gentleman architect, for the 1st Earl of Hardwicke, but not built until twenty years later with modifications by Capability Brown, the landscape designer, and James Essex, a Cambridge architect. Unlike many follies it had a practical purpose, the tower having been built as a gamekeeper's house – could it have symbolised his role as a guardian of the estate? Whatever its purpose, the gamekeeper's house eventually fell out of use and into dereliction, so this artificial ruin is now a real ruin!

The ruined castle, built as a folly at Wimpole Hall. (*Cambridgeshire Collection, Cambridge Central Library*)

The derelict castle folly in the grounds of Wimpole Hall. (*Author's collection*)

5 CHURCHES

The most famous churches in Cambridgeshire are Ely Cathedral, Peterborough Cathedral and King's College Chapel. Ely's great glories include the Lady Chapel and central lantern tower. These were conceived by Alan of Walsingham, who took office as Sacristan in 1314, and was responsible for maintaining the cathedral building. When the central tower collapsed in 1321 Alan decided to replace it with an octagonal structure in which a hidden network of beams suspends a central lantern 92ft above the ground.

The construction of the Lady Chapel was delegated to a monk named John of Wisbech. Just as the money was about to run out, a pot containing a hoard of coins was unearthed on the site. John hid the hoard under his bed and used it to pay the workmen. The building was completed in 1349. It is the largest Lady Chapel in the world, standing 46ft wide and 110ft long, and features the widest single-span stone vaulted roof in Britain.

Aerial view of Ely Cathedral, showing the scale of the Lady Chapel (front left) and the lantern (centre).
(*Author's collection*)

The lantern at Ely Cathedral: weighing over 80 tons, this has been suspended above the centre of the cathedral for more than 600 years. (*Author's collection*)

Romanesque (or Norman) archway at the west end of Ely Cathedral: the weight of the west tower has caused this round arch to bulge and buckle, but it continues to support the structure. (*Author's collection*)

Plan of the maze beneath the west tower of Ely Cathedral. (*Author's collection*)

When Ely Cathedral was being restored in 1870, George Gilbert Scott, the supervising architect, devised a maze which was laid out on the floor tiles below the west tower. It contains a single path 215ft long, the exact height of the tower.

Peterborough Cathedral

Most people visiting Peterborough Cathedral will be struck by the towering west front, with its three 80ft arches. Some architectural historians have argued that this is the most beautiful façade of any church in Europe. The central arch tilts forward, protruding 32in out of vertical at the apex. Had this been caused by external factors (such as the foundations settling), cracks and fissures might have appeared in the walls, yet there is no sign of these. Evidently the masons building it realised that if the columns stood vertically they would appear to converge as they rose, and the lean was deliberately made to rectify this.

A statue of St Peter stands at the apex of the central gable. At the base of the west door's central column is a carving of a man falling headlong to the ground, surrounded by demons. This is Simon Magus, who appears in chapter eight of the Acts of the Apostles in the New Testament. An accomplished magician, when Simon saw the apostles perform miracles he offered to pay Peter for the secret of their power − hence the expression 'simony', meaning to buy or sell ecclesiastical offices. A medieval legend said that Simon met his end when he tried to fly, and this carving depicts his downfall.

Work on the present cathedral began in 1118. The central tower was built between 1160 and 1170, and like many churches of the time it employed round (Romanesque or Norman)

The west front of Peterborough Cathedral. (*Author's collection*)

The downfall of Simon Magus,
St Peter's supposed rival, at the base of
the west front of Peterborough Cathedral.
(*Author's collection*)

arches. However, from the mid-twelfth century masons had abandoned round arches in favour of pointed (Gothic) arches, which could support greater weight. By 1883 the central tower was in danger of collapse, and the architect John Loughborough Pearson rebuilt two tower arches in the pointed Gothic style, a brilliant modern application of a medieval building principle to save a medieval cathedral.

King's College Chapel, Cambridge

Henry VI laid the first stone of King's College Chapel in 1446, but it was not completed until Henry VIII's reign. Although Henry VIII never visited Cambridge, he financed the production of stained glass for twenty-four side windows and the east window. His death in 1547 deprived the west window of stained glass (which was not added until 1879). Nevertheless, the chapel contains the world's largest display of Renaissance stained glass in its original setting. The fourth window from the west on the north wall is worth a special inspection: the lower lights show Christ's circumcision by a doctor wearing pince-nez glasses, the earliest representation of spectacles in art. The upper lights show King Solomon, modelled on Henry VIII himself. Perhaps this was appropriate, since both kings were famous for their many wives.

King's College Chapel from the south. (*Author's collection*)

Great St Mary's, Cambridge

It is only possible to describe a small fraction of the county's other historic churches here. Great St Mary's, which faces Market Hill in Cambridge, is the university church: its tower is the centre of the town and the university. Construction of the present tower began in 1491, but the Reformation interrupted the work and it wasn't completed until 1608. In the same years John Warren, the churchwarden overseeing the project, fell from the battlements to his death, an event commemorated by a plaque beside the nave entry.

Plans to add a spire failed for lack of funds, but soon this could be remedied: at time of writing, the Eyecone Project to build the 80ft spire is underway. The project was initiated by Issam Khorbaj, artist in residence at Christ's College, who one day was amazed to see a Cambridge street scene projected like a film onto his studio wall. A hole in his curtain had created a camera obscura (Latin for 'dark room') effect. Intrigued by this, Issam considered installing a permanent camera obscura in Cambridge. He thought the tower of Great St Mary's might be an ideal location for such a scheme, especially after discovering that it was meant to possess a spire. It is hoped that the spire, containing a camera obscura showing all Cambridge, will be in place by 2008, for the 800th anniversary of the inception of the university.

Great St Mary's contains a mobile pulpit on rails, so the preacher can be moved to a more prominent and visible place during university sermons. In 1793 Joseph Jowett, Regius Professor of Civil Law, composed a tune for the clock chimes based on Handel's 'I Know That My Redeemer Liveth'. This was used by the clock of the Houses of Parliament in 1859, to become famous as Westminster Chimes. Before the altar there is a floor memorial the leading Protestant thinker, Martin Bucer, who became Regius Professor of Divinity at Cambridge in 1549 but died two years later. From 1553 Queen Mary Tudor initiated a programme to extirpate Protestantism and in 1557 Bucer's remains were exhumed and burnt for heresy on Market Hill. A plausible explanation may be that the university authorities wished to obey royal decrees and decided this was more expedient than burning living people! Bucer's admirers collected his ashes. These were reburied in Great St Mary's in 1560; he was thus buried twice!

Ramsey Parish Church

At Ramsey the church lies near the abbey gatehouse, adjoining the road to the north and west. Although Ramsey Abbey was founded in 963, the town of Ramsey was slow to develop: it is not mentioned in Domesday Book and there is no record of a parish church there until 1291. It is widely believed that this church was built as the abbey guesthouse, to accommodate pilgrims and travellers, and only converted into a parish church after the town developed – an unusual survival of a building of this type.

Swaffham Prior

At Swaffham Prior two churches stand in one churchyard: St Cyriac and Julitta's and St Mary's. In 1800 John Peter Allix, the Lord of the Manor, commissioned Charles Humfrey, a Cambridge architect, to rebuild St Cyriac and Julitta's (apart from the fifteenth-century tower).

St Mary's twelfth-century tower has a square base that recedes into an octagon (the earliest use of this construction technique in Britain), while the third storey further recedes into a sixteen-sided structure. John Peter Allix planned to demolish St Mary's for its stone,

Ramsey Church. (*Author's collection*)

View across the churchyard showing the two churches at Swaffham Prior.
(*Cambridgeshire Collection, Cambridge Central Library*)

THOUGH ° THEY ° CLIMB ° UP ° TO ° HEAVEN °
THENCE ° WILL ° I ° BRING ° THEM ° DOWN ° AMOS IX.2

Detail of the war memorial window in St Mary's Church at Swaffham Prior, designed by the Allix family, showing a German war plane (actually a French Spad war plane with German markings). Could the text be an ironical protest at the horrors of war? (*Reproduced by permission of the Vicar of Swaffham Prior*)

but his death in 1807 saved it from total destruction, and in 1902 it was restored for use as a church. St Cyriac's was then abandoned, but is now cared for by the Churches Conservation Trust. The Allix family designed stained glass for St Mary's. Local tradition recalls how they covered the billiard table at Swaffham Hall with pictures of possible subjects, while searching the Bible for texts. Two Benedicite windows, or 'a hymn of praise in glass', illustrate such subjects as a glacier, Mount Pilatus in Switzerland, the 1771 eruption of Vesuvius and Wicken Fen.

There are three war-memorial windows: one shows inventions of war, including a munitions factory, a howitzer, flame-throwers, a tank, a warplane and a Zeppelin. Another shows ways to relieve the horrors of war, such as a field hospital, a YMCA hut and a chaplain ministering to troops. The third shows benefits of peace, such as agriculture and industry. This representation of the horrors of warfare was controversial, and there were complaints that it took the phrase 'war memorial' rather too literally.

March's spectacular angel roof. (*Author's collection*)

Angel roofs at March and Willingham

From the fifteenth century many East Anglian church roof beams were decorated with angels. March possesses England's most ornate 'Angel roof', with a record-breaking host of 118, along with over 2,000 fleurs-de-lys (plus a spoiler: a deliberate error in the form of a little devil hidden in a dark corner), whose impact cannot easily be imagined without a visit to the church.

Willingham contains an elaborate angel roof, although the beams do not align with the rest of the building, nor do the windows light it very well. There was a tradition that it came from Barnwell Priory, near Cambridge. In 1890 John Watkins, the new rector, found that the apex of the roof had been cut off to narrow it, and the date 1613 was carved into the beams, suggesting it had indeed been moved from elsewhere at some point in the seventeenth century.

Old Church, Guyhirn

The Old Church at Guyhirn, which bears the date 1660 on the door lintel, was built for a Protestant congregation, probably French and Walloon refugees who settled in the area. Wooden benches inside were designed for Puritan religious observance, which

Guyhirn's Old Church. The finely cut stone may have been reused from Thorney Abbey nearby.
(*Author's collection*)

encouraged long sermons, but forbade kneeling to pray: thus they are close together, to prevent sitters kneeling, and have high, straight backs to help attentiveness. Services ended in Victorian times, but Donald Dickinson, a local clergyman, formed a friends' group with the poet Sir John Betjeman's support to rescue it from dereliction. Placed in the care of the Churches Conservation Trust in 1973, it has now been restored to its early austere splendour.

Bourn Church

The spire at Bourn has twisted out of shape because of the warping of the supporting timbers. Underneath, on the tower floor, there is a tile maze, laid between 1873 and 1875, possibly inspired by the turf mazes at Hilton and Comberton (Bourn lies midway between these villages). Its layout copies the hedge maze at Hampton Court, and is thus unique among ecclesiastical floor mazes as a genuine puzzle maze, where one could get lost negotiating the path. The font stands at the centre, perhaps symbolising the newly baptised Christian's journey through life.

Bourn Church's unique tile maze. (*Author's collection*)

Bourn Church: note the crooked spire. (*Cambridgeshire Collection, Cambridge Central Library*)

Sacred Heart, St Ives

The Roman Catholic Church of the Sacred Heart in St Ives was moved from Cambridge. Designed for the Cambridge Roman Catholic congregation by Augustus Welby Northmore Pugin, England's leading pioneer of the Gothic Revival, it was consecrated and dedicated to St Andrew in 1843: the first Roman Catholic church to be built in Cambridgeshire since the Reformation. Standing in Union Road, it was superseded by the present Church of Our

Design for the New Catholic Church of St Andrew, Cambridge

Augustus Welby
Pugin's designs for
St Andrew's Roman
Catholic church in
Cambridge.
*(Cambridgeshire Collection,
Cambridge Central Library)*

St Ives Roman
Catholic church.
(Author's collection)

Lady and The English Martyrs in 1890. In 1902 George Pauling, a prominent member of the St Ives Roman Catholic community, had it dismantled and transported to St Ives by barge to be rebuilt in Needingworth Road.

All Saints', Cambridge

All Saints' in Cambridge, designed in 1863 by G.F. Bodley, is a little altered example of an influential High Anglican Gothic church in the care of the Churches Conservation Trust. In the 1870s the interior was covered with wall paintings by Frederick Richard Leach, a local craftsman, and Wyndham Hope Hughes, to recreate the appearance of a medieval church. A painting of St Peter on the pulpit was modelled on Herbert Luckock, the first vicar. The east window was designed by the Pre-Raphaelites, including William Morris, who portrayed himself as St Peter (and may have modelled St Catherine on his wife, Jane Burden). The 'Women's Window' was designed in 1944 in memory of Louisa Murrish, a

The Women's Window at All Saints' Church, Cambridge, showing John the Baptist as a Boy Scout (left), and the artist's dog (right). (*Author's collection*)

Pulpit panel at All Saints' Church, Cambridge, portraying Herbert Luckock, the first Vicar, as St Peter. (*Author's collection*)

parishioner. As a former member of the 12th Cambridge Scout Troop, Louisa's husband, John Murrish, asked that a boy scout be included: he was modelled by George William ('Bill') Hames, the troop's patrol leader. Douglas Strachan, the artist, included his Irish Wolfhound, Eilan, in the design.

Carvings and sculptures

Strange carvings and sculptures are among the most intriguing features of Cambridgeshire churches. Castor contains some of England's most elaborate Romanesque sculpture, including a Latin inscription recording its consecration in 1124: one of the first churches in England whose building date is recorded architecturally.

The font at St Peter's Church, Cambridge.
(*Author's collection*)

Stonework on the central tower at Castor.
(*Author's collection*)

A tympanum (recessed space over a door) at Little Paxton shows a man holding a staff and two small animals being menaced by a larger beast. The man may be Jesus as the good shepherd; the smaller animals may be Christians represented as sheep; while the larger beast could be the Devil as a ravening wolf. A mermaid appears on a tympanum at Stow Longa, although her wild posture does not look very seductive. Four mermen with forked tails are carved on the twelfth-century font at St Peter's Church in Cambridge, cared for by the Churches Conservation Trust. As mermen live in water they may represent baptism, or show Christ's dual nature as God and man.

On the south wall of Godmanchester there is a thirteenth-century sundial, or mass dial, divided into eight segments, marking the Anglo-Saxon division of morning and afternoon into eight ninety-minute periods. A sculpture on the lintel of a tower window at Whittlesford shows a naked man with a distended phallus and a 'Sheela Na Gig' figure, a contorted naked woman, which has been resued from an older building. It is uncertain why masons would place such lewd caricatures on a church. Suggestions that they are fertility spirits hardly accord with their extreme ugliness: they may represent the evils of lust.

The Green Man, a strange, ferocious foliage-covered face, is a ubiquitous artistic motif. He probably had several meanings, including being a symbol of the wild, of the natural world, of order and disorder, a guardian spirit or man's primeval nature. A twelfth-century example, one of the earliest in Britain, was found in the south wall at Grantchester in 1877 and placed on the exterior of the church. A roof corbel (or support) in Holywell (thus named for the holy well in the churchyard) displays a vividly painted example. Sometimes he appears on fonts: as at Bluntisham, where he peers through the door; Tydd St Giles,

Whittlesford
carvings.
(*Author's collection*)

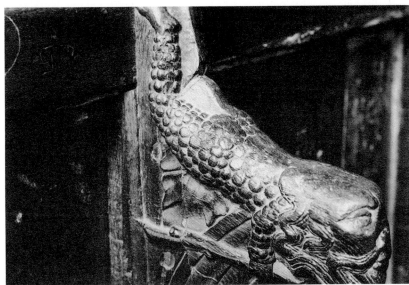

A 'Wodewose' or
Wild Man on
the choir stalls
at Balsham.
(*Author's collection*)

Wild Man at St Botolph's Church guarding the approaches to Cambridge. (*Cambridgeshire Collection, Cambridge Central Library*)

where he fills one side panel and hides among carvings on a second; or Trumpington, where three surround the base. Others can be found on misericords (tilt-up seats) in choir stalls at Over and the armrests of choir stalls at Swavesey and Balsham. Landbeach displays six on the roof woodwork and two beside the exterior of the east window. He peeks over the edge of the roof vault in the porch of St John the Baptist in Peterborough, the entrance door inside the west porch at Peterborough Cathedral and the entrance to the north-east side chapel in King's College Chapel. A very fine representation appears in the arcading in the Lady Chapel at Ely Cathedral, west of the entrance passage. At St Botolph's in Cambridge a shaggy 'Wodewose' or Wild Man sits on the tower, looking down Trumpington Street and Silver Street; perhaps he is meant to guard the southern approach to the town.

Wall paintings

The interiors of most medieval churches were decorated with wall paintings, few of which now survive. However, after an arsonist had set fire to Ickleton Church in 1979 the restoration revealed twelfth-century frescoes (scenes painted onto plaster before it dried) showing the Passion of Jesus and the martyrdoms of saints. Their use of this medium and early date, along with their artistic quality, place them among the earliest and most artistically significant wall paintings anywhere in England. Willingham contains paintings from the thirteenth to the eighteenth centuries and a screen there is decorated with

Above: Twelfth-century fresco at Ickleton showing the Last Supper (above) and the martyrdom of St Peter (below, partly obscured by a memorial). St Peter was crucified upside down; his head is obscured by a Victorian wall plaque. (*Author's collection*)

Above: Popinjays on medieval screen at Willingham. (*Author's collection*)

Left: Wall painting of St Thomas Becket at Hauxton. (*Cambridgeshire Collection, Cambridge Central Library*)

popinjays. When a bricked-up medieval window at Hauxton was reopened in the nineteenth century a painting of St Thomas Becket was found on the window jamb. Henry VIII held a particular dislike of Thomas Becket, and took special steps to obliterate his cult; this window had been blocked before Henry VIII's reign, hiding the image from Reformation iconoclasts.

Leaning towers

Some churches show structural faults: the tower at Stilton leans westward, possibly because the foundations have settled. Yet it contains a peal of bells, and the residents of the adjacent vicarage are not intimidated by it. The tower at Elm also leans westwards, probably owing to the instability of the Fen soil or foundations. But for crookedness St Mark's Church at Friday Bridge is hard to beat. Built in 1864, it has sunk into the Fen soil and tilts to the north; the Victorian Rectory, north of the churchyard, is nearly as remarkable, as this tilts to the south. The church has been dubbed by some The Leaning Tower of Pisa of the Fens. The walk from the altar to the tilting west window can be somewhat disconcerting, and it is not just because of the communion wine!

Friday Bridge Church, the 'Leaning Tower of Pisa of the Fens'. Its angle of tilt is greater then that of the Pisan tower. (*Reproduced by permission of the Vicar of Elm and Friday Bridge*)

Monument, believed to
be of a forester, at
Glinton. (*Author's collection*)

Monuments, memorials and ruins

Some church memorials tell unusual stories. In the porch at Glinton there are two very
worn medieval memorials to a man and a woman; evidently they came from elsewhere,
and were left outdoors for many years before being placed here. As the man carries a horn
it has been suggested that he was a forester. Oliver Cromwell's son Henry retired to Wicken
after the Civil War. On his death in 1673 he was buried in the church under a simple black
floor slab north of the altar, the only surviving contemporary memorial to any member of

Left: The Washington memorial at Little St Mary's Church, Cambridge. Commemorating George Washington's great-uncle, Godfrey Washington, it shows the Washington family coat of arms, which may have been the inspiration for the stars and stripes on the US national flag. (*Reproduced by permission of the Vicar and churchwardens of Little St Mary's*)
Right: The ruins of Silverley Church. (*Author's collection*)

the Cromwell family. Great St Andrew's in Cambridge contains the earliest memorial to Captain James Cook, the eighteenth-century explorer, paid for by his wife Elizabeth, who was buried here near two of her sons.

A wall tablet at Little St Mary's in Cambridge commemorates George Washington's great-uncle, Godfrey Washington, who was vicar there. The monument includes the Washington family coat of arms, which has been suggested as a possible inspiration for the design of the US national flag.

Silverley Church, near Newmarket, is one of the county's few true ruins. In the thirteenth century Silverley merged with the neighbouring village of Ashley, leaving the church in isolation. Money was left to build the tower between 1517 and 1528, but the church became a barn after the Reformation. Most of the building had vanished by the eighteenth century, but the tower was so strongly built that it resisted all efforts to remove it – even a misguided demolition attempt in 1971!

The Fenland Ark

Cambridgeshire's most unusual church may have been St Withburga's at Holme, known as the Fenland Ark. When Horatio Broke became vicar of Holme in 1895 he found many roads impassable during bad weather. Horatio (a suitably naval name) realised there were 9 miles of waterways in his parish which could be navigated by small craft. He commissioned William Starling, a Stanground boat builder, to build a houseboat. The cabin was consecrated as a church and dedicated to St Withburga (an East Anglian princess enshrined at Ely). Three horses – Nancy, Yeast and Sam – pulled St Withburga's to waterside settlements. Baptisms and communions were popular, although a technicality in ecclesiastical regulations prevented marriages. Some local girls formed a choir, and Mrs Broke ran women's classes on board. In 1897 the church was featured in the *Strand Magazine* (which introduced Sherlock Holmes to the world).

By 1904 the novelty of a floating church was fading and Horatio's health was deteriorating. St Withburga's was sailed to Manea, where the Revd Frederic Godfrey Guy used her to minister to remote parishioners. When she began to deteriorate she was sold to some young men who renamed her the Saints' Rest. In 1912 she was allowed to sink; her benches and lectern are kept at Holme and Stilton.

Village sign at Holme, showing the Fenland Ark, the parish's floating church. (*Author's collection*)

6 WHERE STREAMS OF LIVING WATERS FLOW

Water is essential to all life, and all settlements need a supply of good drinking water. Thus springs and wells, especially those possessing unusual features, have long been regarded as landmarks or sacred spots.

The red waters of Knapwell

The village name Knapwell means 'Red Well'. It is so called from a spring that rises over an iron-ore deposit that lies in Overhall Grove, a nature reserve in the parish. Although somewhat difficult to find, as it is some distance from the footpath and its location is not signposted, the water rising from the spring still contains distinct red sediments.

Holywell spring

Holywell derives its name from a spring on the south of the churchyard, which must have been regarded as sacred in the Middle Ages, since Domesday Book recorded the village as

The well at Holywell. (*Author's collection*)

Eltisley Church, built next to (the now lost) St Pandonia's Well.
(Cambridgeshire Collection, Cambridge Central Library)

'Haliwell' in 1086. Samuel Beckwith, the Rector, had a brick canopy built over it in 1845. Well-dressing ceremonies are now held here in June, to coincide with the festival of the church's patron saint, John the Baptist (an appropriate saint for a church with a holy well).

St Pandonia's Well

St Pandonia's Well stood beside Eltisley Church. John Leland, a sixteenth-century antiquarian and historian visited Eltisley, where he saw an account of Pandonia's life, which described her as the daughter of a Scottish king who fled several suitors to found a nunnery at Eltisley. She was buried by her well, but in 1344 her remains were moved into the church. Pandonia's hagiography was probably displayed in the church, but it has long since been lost; although it seems plausible that this attributed healing powers and miracle cures to her well, we cannot now know any details.

Robert Palmer, who was appointed Vicar of Eltisley in 1575, destroyed the well's stone surround. Summoned before the consistory court, he said, 'It was a well used for superstitious purposes, therefore he brake it down.' Given the spirit of the post-Reformation age diocesan officials were not concerned at the desecration of a sacred spring: they were alarmed that the removal of the stone surround had created a safety hazard. Robert Palmer was not the most conscientious clergyman: he was also charged with using his vicarage as an alehouse, breaking church pavements and letting cattle into the church! His neglect of the church probably led to the loss of Pandonia's well, which has vanished without trace.

The lost spring at St Ives

In AD 1000 a stone coffin (probably Roman) containing a skeleton was found near a village called Slepe. The remains were identified as Ivo, a long forgotten (and previously unknown) saint, and Slepe was renamed St Ives. A spring rose at the spot. This may have been due to soil disturbance, but the spring's waters were soon believed to possess miraculous healing powers; it could even be seen as a manifestation of the symbolic power of a hero as a bringer of water.

A priory was built over the site to house Ivo's remains. At the dedication three blind people regained their sight after washing their eyes with water from the spring, and some monks, including Eadnoth, the Abbot of Ramsey, used the water to cure their illnesses. The wall of the priory church was built over the spring so pilgrims could visit it without disturbing the monks. The priory was destroyed after the Dissolution in 1536, so the spring has long been lost.

Longstanton's Holy Spring

A spring in the churchyard of St Michael's church at Longstanton was covered by a brick canopy in 1884. This was saved from dereliction in 1985 by two villagers, Arthur and Phyllis Brown, and is now well kept.

The chalybeate springs

Several chalybeate springs (containing iron salts) acquired a reputation for medicinal properties in more recent times, and were the centre of schemes to create spas, where people could drink (or bathe in) the waters to relieve illnesses and improve their health.

In 1586, William Harrison, an Essex clergyman, wrote a *Description of England* in which he said two springs had recently been discovered at Hail Weston: 'Never went people so fast from the church, either unto a fair or market, as they go to these wells.' Water from one tasted sweet and fresh and was said to be good for eye diseases; water from the other, which tasted brackish and salty, was efficacious for skin complaints. Perhaps their fame was due to the fact that they had such different tastes, even though they were so close together.

Michael Drayton's *Poly Olbion*, a Jacobean fantasy poem providing a mythical origin for the natural features of the British Isles, said that the Hail Weston Springs were nymphs who pined away for unrequited love and were turned to springs. In 1844 a Hail Weston Springs Company bought the wells to bottle the water for commercial sale. The operation continued until 1954, employing about six people, but was then abandoned, and the area turned over to agriculture.

A chalybeate spring at Somersham was ambitiously promoted. Samuel Knight, Rector of Bluntisham, discovered the spring at the start of the eighteenth century and initiated a determined scheme to develop it as a spa. A bathhouse was built and a bowling green laid out. Evidently Samuel Knight intended the spa to be a social and recreational centre. Thomas Addenbrooke, the physician and founder of Cambridge's Addenbrooke's Hospital, bottled the water and took it to Cambridge, saying that it was efficacious for many ailments. Unfortunately two patients taking the water for kidney, or gallstones, died. Interest rapidly evaporated (to coin an appropriate phrase); the bathhouse was demolished and the bowling green left to grow over. Daniel Layard attempted to revive Somersham Spa. Born in 1721, Layard was one of the most prominent physicians of the day, studying and practising medicine in Britain and France, before moving to Huntingdon in 1750. (He later became physician to the royal family.) Dr Layard took a great interest in the Somersham springs. He performed experiments on the water, analysing its mineral content and chemical properties, which he published in the *Philosophical Transactions* of the Royal Society, the leading scientific and intellectual journal of the day.

He then leased the land on which the spring and the old bathhouse stood, and formed a proprietary club (privately owned and run for profit) to develop it. An appeal for subscriptions was answered by thirty-seven people, including local clergymen, medical practitioners, landowners and Fellows of several Cambridge colleges. An elaborate bathhouse was built, but the spa failed to attract the eagerly anticipated hordes of visitors. Dr Layard left Huntingdon in 1762, and in 1820 a history of Huntingdon wrote that Somersham Spa was but little regarded.

By the twentieth century only the foundations of the bathhouse remained, and these were ploughed up when a farmer planted fruit trees on the site. There is nothing now to show where the spa stood, and few people in Somersham are even aware of its existence.

Cowper's Spring

Cowper's Spring on Spring Common at Huntingdon enjoyed some popularity in the eighteenth century. It is named after William Cowper, the poet, who thought highly of it when he lived in Huntingdon. In 1875 a bathhouse for the use of local residents was built over it, although more as a venture in public hygiene than as a spa. With improvements in domestic plumbing and the building of new public amenities the bathhouse passed out of use and was demolished, but the spring can still be seen.

Longthorpe Holy Well

Longthorpe Holy Well was a popular recreational spot. A natural spring in the grounds of Thorpe Hall, it was converted into an elaborate garden ornament, probably by Sir John Bernard, who acquired the hall by marriage in 1756. A grotto was built over it, and a pool and fishponds were fed from its water. Stories about its antiquity circulated: it was said to have been the residence of 'St Cloud', a medieval holy man, and a centre of pilgrimage, although there is no record of the spring before the eighteenth century.

The well was a popular destination for ramblers and promenaders in the nineteenth century, and a local clergyman, the Revd A.J. Scrimshare, built a lavender and peppermint distillery there. Three nearby houses were called Holy Water Cottages, and the 1861 census recorded one occupant called Fielding as a 'lavender distiller'. The spot eventually fell out of fashion. The buildings above the well were demolished as a result 'of the disorderly proceedings of the visitors from Peterborough', and the remains are now overgrown and neglected.

St Neots spa scheme

In the late nineteenth century there was a final effort to develop a spa at St Neots. A chalybeate spring near the paper mill stood on a small platform approached by some steps. Nothing is known of its history before 1895, when a local entrepreneur called J. McNish set up a committee which leased it, dug a new 90ft bore, and began to promote it. The scheme was accompanied by some of the most elaborate civic fanfare in the town's history.

Fydell Rowley, a scion of the town's wealthiest family, officially opened the new well on Whit Monday, when thirty boats rowed from St Neots Bridge to the spa with a band of musicians on board. The town's football club, which had just won the Fellows Cup, drank to the venture's success from its newly acquired trophy. Stories circulated that a dog had been cured of sores by bathing in the water. Jordan & Addington, a local company, announced that it would bottle and sell the water under the name Neotia. There were plans to open a pump room, and it was confidently anticipated that St Neots would grow to rival Harrogate and Cheltenham.

Alas, the venture met with little success. No land was available on which to build a pump house. Moreover, many people complained that the water tasted unpleasant, and by 1900 the scheme had dissolved into nothing (metaphorically and perhaps literally), when people condemned the spa as a neglected eyesore.

Cambridgeshire water supplies

Cambridgeshire contains some historic water supplies and, although no miraculous or curative properties have been claimed for them, they are among the earliest functioning examples of their kind in Britain.

The county's oldest man-made water supply is a large well in the centre of the cloister court at Peterborough Cathedral. Anglo-Saxon stonework and masonry has been found at the bottom of the bore, and it is thought that this was dug in 654 for the first Christian community to be established on the site. The well continued as the principal source of

Trinity College fountain. (*Author's collection*)

Monument to Andrew Perne, Thomas Hobson and other benefactors of Cambridge's first water supply at the Nine Wells at Great Shelford. (*Cambridgeshire Collection, Cambridge Central Library*)

Hobson's Conduit in its present location, at the head of Hobson's Brook.
(*Cambridgeshire Collection, Cambridge Central Library*)

drinking water for the monks and the cathedral clergy until the introduction of mains water to Peterborough.

The Franciscan Friars of Cambridge, whose convent stood on the site of Sidney Sussex College, built a water supply in 1327. They laid a pipe to carry water from a spring called Bradrusshe, in the north-west part of Cambridge, under the River Cam to their convent, a distance of 2,370yd. This was also a public water supply; until the sixteenth century Sidney Street was called Conduit Street. King's Hall College was allowed to share the Franciscans' water supply. After the Dissolution the Franciscans' convent was demolished and its water supply lost, but Henry VIII incorporated King's Hall into his new foundation of Trinity College, where the conduit still supplies the fountain in the Great Court.

A later practical experiment in public sanitation and water supply was devised in 1574, after a plague outbreak killed 100 people in Cambridge. It was recognised that one of the causes was the fetid, refuse-filled King's Ditch, the Anglo-Saxon town ditch on the east side of the town, which had degenerated into a public refuse tip. Andrew Perne, the Master of Peterhouse, suggested that a supply of clean water should be channelled from outside the town to simultaneously flush out the ditch and provide a supply of fresh water. He suggested that a group of springs on the other side of Trumpington, known as the Nine Wells, would be ideal for this purpose. Andrew Perne's scheme was not acted upon until 1610, when Thomas Delapole, a Trumpington landowner, allowed a watercourse to be built over his land. An open channel carried water to a conduit head at the corner of the modern Trumpington Road and Lensfield Road, from where it was piped underground into the King's Ditch. Additional culverts supplied water for Peterhouse and Pembroke Colleges until the eighteenth century.

In 1614 a second underground pipe was drawn from the conduit head to Market Hill to feed a public fountain, which became Cambridge's principal drinking-water supply. A large ornamental stone edifice was placed over the fountain, not just to beautify it but also to stop people from dirtying or fouling the water. The Corporation arranged for it to run red wine for Charles II's coronation in 1661 and royal visits in 1671, 1689 and 1705, which does sound like a great extravagance, although on the last three occasions wine may only have been pumped as the King passed by.

A third watercourse was cut in 1631, running south from the conduit head to a point just past the modern Roman Catholic church, and then north-west along St Andrew's Street as far as Christ's College. A stream ran from this into Emmanuel College, to feed the college's fishponds and bath, and then into Christ's College, to fill the Master's pond.

Perhaps the most interesting part of the experiment are the runnels that lead into the road to flush out the gutters. The first stage of the scheme included two channels which directed small streams of water along the gutters of Trumpington Street, to keep the road clean and wash away dirt and debris. When the scheme was extended into St Andrew's Street two more runnels were installed to flush out the gutters there. These have run regularly ever since, a fascinating and unique exercise in public hygiene and sanitation.

When a modern waterworks company was started in Cambridge in 1855 the fountain cover was moved from the market to the conduit head in Trumpington Street, where it can still be seen.

This water supply has since been identified with Thomas Hobson, the famous Cambridge tradesman. The conduit head and the water supply in general are often called

Hobson's Conduit, while the stream from Trumpington is called Hobson's Brook. Although the scheme was not Thomas Hobson's idea, and it is uncertain that he played any role in setting it up, he did leave generous benefactions for its maintenance in his will. The name may derive from the fact that Thomas Hobson was the town's most famous sixteenth-century resident. (As at St Ives, it may be an aspect of the role of the hero as a water bringer.) The walk from the conduit head along Hobson's Brook is an attractive public footpath, finishing at Great Shelford at the Nine Wells, where an obelisk displays inscriptions outlining the scheme's history.

7 RIDDLES IN THE LANDSCAPE

Cambridgeshire contains many ancient earthworks which have puzzled archaeologists and historians. During the Iron Age East Anglia was the domain of the Iceni, famous for their rebellion against the Romans under Boudicca. Iron Age peoples defined their power and territory by constructing hill forts. Stonea Camp, near March, was first dug in 200 BC on a Fen island. Standing only 6ft above sea level, it is Britain's lowest lying hill fort. Another hill fort, known as Belsar's Hill, at Willingham, covers the Aldreth Causeway, a route to the Isle of Ely. It has been suggested that William the Conqueror used it as a base against Hereward the Wake.

Wandlebury Iron Age Fort

The most prominent hill fort in Cambridgeshire is Wandlebury, on the Gogmagog Hills (or 'The Gogs', as they are known locally), the county's highest natural point, 234ft above sea level. Wandlebury is a nearly circular earthwork about 1,000ft in diameter overlooking the Icknield Way. Archaeological excavations suggest that a single ditch and rampart, topped by a timber fence, were dug between the fourth and first centuries BC. These were allowed to

The ramparts at Wandlebury. (*Author's collection*)

collapse, but at about the start of the Christian era they were reconstructed, when a higher, inner bank with another ditch was dug, before being abandoned in early Roman times.

In 1976 a tree on the hillside was blown down, uncovering five adult skeletons, hastily buried in a shallow depression. One had had the chin chopped off, as if by a sword. Perhaps they died in an unsuccessful attack, or in defence of the earthworks. It was once thought that Wandlebury guarded the approach into the Iceni's territory. Yet if the ramparts had a purely military purpose they should have touched the hillside: in fact they lie away from the summit and fail to use its contours. It has now been suggested that the site could have been a ritual centre. In 1685 Sidney, the 1st Earl of Godolphin, built a hunting lodge in the earthworks. His son Francis, the 2nd Earl, replaced this with a mansion, levelling the interior ditch and rampart to create a garden. In 1953, after a public fund-raising campaign, the Gogs were acquired by the Cambridge Preservation Society to become a widely enjoyed public park and recreation area.

The name Wandlebury means Waendel's Burgh (enclosure): Waendel, or Wandil, was a Norse God, often associated with high places, who was popular in early Anglo-Saxon times. Gog and Magog appear in chapters 38 and 39 of Ezekiel and in Revelations 20:8 – by Elizabethan times they had acquired legendary significance, featuring in Edmund Spenser's *Fairie Queen* as the chief giants of Albion. The history of the area has been confused by stories of a lost hill figure. In about 1640 John Layer, a Cambridgeshire antiquary, mentioned 'a high and mighty portraiture of a giant which the scholars of Cambridge cut upon the turf or superficies of the earth within the said trench'. The travel diary of Dr Samuel Dale, an eighteenth-century physician, mentions the 'gigantic figure at Gog Magog cut in the middle camp'. The Revd William Cole, the Cambridgeshire historian, wrote that when he was a boy in the 1720s, his parents would show him 'the figure of a giant carved on the turf'.

Thomas Charles (better known as T.C.) Lethbridge courted controversy by his efforts to rediscover the hill figure. A graduate of Trinity College and an experienced and distinguished Cambridgeshire archaeologist, in 1955 he was asked to help direct an

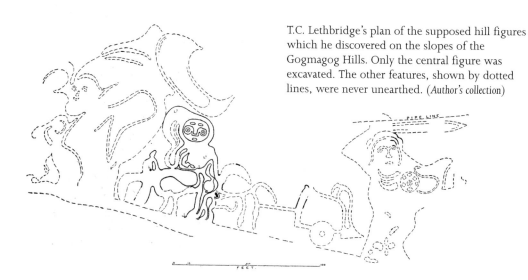

T.C. Lethbridge's plan of the supposed hill figures which he discovered on the slopes of the Gogmagog Hills. Only the central figure was excavated. The other features, shown by dotted lines, were never unearthed. (*Author's collection*)

excavation at Wandlebury. Having heard of a tradition that the hill figure was visible from Sawston, he abandoned the excavation to search for the figure by probing the hillside with a steel rod. Over eight months he made 40,000 soundings, and found not one, but three figures. His discoveries created an immediate furore: the overwhelming majority of his fellow archaeologists (many of whom visited his investigations) roundly denounced his techniques and methodology as unsound, and the Cambridge Preservation Society refused him permission to continue his work.

Lethbridge abandoned archaeology in high dudgeon and devoted the rest of his life to psychic research. Subsequent investigations have been wholly unfavourable to T.C. Lethbridge's investigations: his soundings, which were based on how the ground felt to his probing, rather than any objective measure of soil disturbance, created a gigantic 'join the dots' puzzle open to many interpretations. Resistivity and magnetometer surveys have found no evidence of soil disturbance, and many cavities and trenches which were identified as part of the figures were caused by natural weathering or animal activity and can be found elsewhere on the hill slope: one key feature of his discovery was a tree bore.

The hill figure's real appearance and archaeological significance remains a mystery. William Camden, the Elizabethan antiquarian mentioned a visit to Wandlebury in his *Britannia*, published in 1586 and often cited as the first guidebook to Britain. He wrote that the earthworks impressed him, yet he fails to mention any hill figure. It therefore seems plausible that the figure was cut by students after his visit. Once cut the figure would have returned to nature without regular maintenance, yet there is no indication that this took place, suggesting that when first described the figure was not of great age. And while descriptions are tantalisingly vague, they could suggest that the figure was cut inside the camp, rather than on the hillside: if so it would have been destroyed when Wandlebury was imparked.

The cleared section of Lethbridge's hill figures was left exposed on the hillside, although it was not publicised in any way. In the last few years it has been allowed to grass over. Although the figures cannot be regarded as monuments of antiquity, they do form an unconventional footnote to the history of British archaeology. An interesting curiosity, they tell an archaeological cautionary tale, so their loss would be genuinely regrettable.

The Bartlow Hills

Seven barrows, or burial mounds, known as the Bartlow Hills, form one of Britain's most impressive archaeological sites. Four conical mounds stand in a row: one is 18ft high and 80ft in diameter; two are 35ft high and roughly 90ft in diameter; the fourth is 45ft high and 140ft in diameter and is the largest and highest barrow in Britain. Three smaller barrows to the south have been eroded by weather and agriculture into comparatively small hillocks.

Busick Harwood, a Cambridge academic, organised some excavations on the Bartlow Hills in 1815, partly to provide work for local unemployed men, but a more thorough investigation was conducted between 1832 and 1840 by John Gage of Hengrave Hall in Suffolk, the Director of the Society of Antiquaries of London. By tunnelling into the hills Gage found that six had been built over wooden chests and one over a small brick chamber. Each contained lamps – between 3 and 12in high, some containing liquid – pottery vessels, glass flasks and burnt human bones. The chamber in the largest mound held a folding

Engraving of Bartlow Hills in 1779 from *The Universal British Traveller*. The engraver has taken the libery of adding an extra hill. (*Cambridgeshire Collection, Cambridge Central Library*)

chair, possibly a symbol of rank or a favoured possession, and there was another smaller interment in a pottery vessel outside the burial chamber. Lamps were to light the soul's journey to the afterlife; liquids may have been for the soul's sustenance or offerings to the gods; other vessels were probably sacrificial goods. One chest contained vegetation identified as box, a symbol of mourning. The absence of weapons suggested that the deceased were civilians rather than soldiers.

Gage was one of the most far-sighted archaeologists of the time, who realised that there was more to archaeology than simply digging up old objects, and that much could be learned about a find's function, purpose and significance if the circumstances of its discovery were recorded and analysed. He had the finds taken to other people for further study, including the scientist Michael Faraday, now regarded as the founder of electrical science, who dated them to the period between the second and third centuries AD.

In 1852 Baron Braybrook excavated foundations of a Roman villa with a hypocaust (underfloor heating system) in an adjoining field; it was possibly the house of the people buried in the hills. Most of the finds were preserved at the home of Lord Maynard, the landowner, at Dunmow, which burnt down in 1847, but some were given to Saffron Walden Museum, where they can still be seen.

Anglo-Saxon dykes and ditches

South-east Cambridgeshire is crossed by four earthwork ramparts: from east to west, The Devils' Dyke, Fleam Dyke, Brent Ditch, and Bran or Heydon Ditch. Facing westwards, they run between the boulder clay slopes on the south-east edge of the county and the Fen Edge,

Fleam Dyke, c. 1930. (Cambridgeshire
Collection, Cambridge Central Library)

Aerial view of the Devil's Dyke at Reach.
(Reproduced by permission of the Cambridgeshire
Archaeological Field Unit)

Bran Ditch in 1917. (*Cambridgeshire Collection, Cambridge Central Library*)

blocking the Icknield Way. Bran Ditch and the Brent Ditch have largely vanished. The Bran Ditch ran for 3¼ miles in a straight line from the Great Moor, the marsh that gave Fowlmere its name, to Heydon, while the Brent Ditch ran for 1½ miles along from the Cam at Pampisford to Hadstock, just over the county boundary in Essex. Fleam Dyke runs for 4½ miles from Fulbourn, where the Little Wilbraham River has been diverted to link with it, to Balsham, and is still 20ft high in parts. The Devil's Dyke runs for 7½ miles from Reach on the Fen Edge, crossing Newmarket Heath in a spectacular fashion, to Woodditton on the boulder-clay uplands. It still stands up to 33ft high and 115ft wide. Reach lies on a promontory extending into the Fens. Had the dyke been dug only a small distance to the west it could have been significantly shorter; it was evidently routed to take advantage of the local geography.

Archaeological excavations of sections of all four dykes have revealed only a few finds: mostly potsherds and skeletal fragments. Radio carbon dating of these suggested that they were dug after AD 330 and before AD 620, probably in the fifth century.

Although the history of Dark Age Britain is a controversial and widely debated topic, the general (but not universal) opinion of historians and archaeologists is that, in the 200 years following Roman withdrawal in AD 410, Eastern England was either colonised by, or adopted the language and customs of, Germanic or Anglo-Saxon intruders, while Western England tried to maintain Romano-British traditions.

The dykes could have been built as a boundary between the Anglo-Saxon and Romano-British regions, to define the borders of the Anglo-Saxon kingdom of East Anglia and deter invasion. Their construction must have been carefully coordinated: it may have taken about

1,000 men a year to dig a mile of the Devil's Dyke, and they had to be supplied with tools and food. Thus it is conceivable that the entire resources of East Anglia were diverted into building the dykes.

Part of the Bran Ditch was called Gallows Gate; it adjoined Hangman's Field. Here in the 1920s and '30s the archaeologist Cyril Fox found about sixty skeletons, mostly adult males, but including youths and two females. (Counting was difficult, as they were mixed together, and some were dismembered.) Most had been beheaded or hanged, and some had been left to decay before burial. This was probably a *cwealmstow*: a cemetery for criminals who were executed there, and whose bodies were displayed before burial. It may have continued in use after the Norman Conquest, as the medieval lords of the manor of Fowlmere had the right to hang thieves.

Mazes

Iron Age, Roman and Anglo-Saxon earthworks may provide archaeologists with puzzles. Cambridgeshire contains some mazes which are of rather more recent origin, and perhaps more amusing, as they were consciously and deliberately made to puzzle the unwary. Turf mazes are unique to England. Normally circular, they contain a single convoluted passage. In most cases their age and origins are a mystery, but the village green at Hilton contains a turf maze whose origins are recorded on a central stone obelisk, which bears a Latin inscription that can be translated as, 'So passes the glory of the world. William Sparrow, gen [probably meaning creator, but possibly also meaning gentleman], born in the year 1641, died aged 88, formed these rings in the year 1660.'

The Sparrow family were yeoman farmers who lived at Park Farm, a seventeenth-century house which stood behind the maze. Falling into decay, Park Farm was demolished shortly after the Second World War. A large plaster coat of arms of King Charles I, dated 1632, was

The Hilton maze. (*Author's collection*)

William Sparrow's inscription on the Hilton maze obelisk. (*Author's collection*)

Diagram of a turf maze, as laid out in the Botanical Gardens at Cambridge, and as could once be seen at Comberton. (The Hilton maze is slightly anomalous, as the central ring has been omitted to accommodate the obelisk.) (*Author's collection*)

Modern maze in the town park at Huntingdon. (*Author's collection*)

The Balsham hedge maze. (Jim Potter)

uncovered there behind panelling in 1939, and is now displayed over the chancel arch in Hilton Church. This suggests that the Sparrow family were Royalists, and that William Sparrow made the maze to celebrate the Restoration of Charles II. He would only have been 18 or 19 at the time.

There was a turf maze called The Mazles at Comberton. Situated by the central crossroads on the village green, it was 50ft in diameter. Every three years the villagers held a feast-day when they recut it. It was first documented in 1836, but even then was considered to be very old. In 1846 it was incorporated into the playground of the village school, where the energies of the schoolchildren wore it down until it was tarred over in 1929. There is now nothing to show where it was.

William Sparrow's sister, Martha, married Barron Britton of Comberton in 1654. (Barron, in this case, was a personal name, not an aristocratic title.) Did the Comberton maze inspire William Sparrow? Did William Sparrow cut them both? Did the Britton family copy William Sparrow's maze? It is unlikely that we will ever know.

In 1994 trainee technicians at the University Botanical Gardens in Cambridge laid out a turf maze as an open-day project. Now called the Grass Maze, it is maintained as a permanent feature. A small, low hedge maze was planted in Huntingdon Town Park in 1995 at the suggestion of Ruth Pugh, a town councillor. It was laid out by the Town Clerk and the Parks Superintendent, Ted Bocking and Dennis Smith, and a cedar tree was later planted in the centre in memory of Princess Diana.

There is an elaborate hedge maze in a private garden at Balsham. Planted by Jim Potter, the proprietor, in 1993, with green and golden yew trees, the design's full intricacy can only be appreciated from an aeroplane or a balloon! It is laid out to form a treble clef with three destinations: a raised central area, and two smaller brick ornaments in the form of French horns. Fortunately for maze enthusiasts, the proprietors open the garden to the public at least one day a year to raise money for charity.

8 INDUSTRY AND ENTERPRISE

Cambridgeshire people have often demonstrated great ingenuity and enterprise, while Cambridge University has created a demand for new technological innovations. Thus the county has made a remarkable contribution to British trade and industry.

The first windmill

Windmills were among the great technological innovations of the Middle Ages, and it is believed that they were invented in Britain. A charter in the British Library's Additional Manuscripts records how Reginald Arsic, the De Vere family's mesne tenant of Silverley in south-east Cambridgeshire between 1166 and 1194, granted the tithes of a windmill there to Hatfield Regis Priory in Essex. This could be the earliest surviving reference to a windmill in the world. Silverley merged with the adjoining village of Ashley in the thirteenth century. The mill stood in the Breach, a field north-east of the present village; Mill Lane runs along the west of the field, and a mill stood at the highest point of the road until the early twentieth century.

Bourn Windmill. Among the oldest standing windmills in England, its history is fully documented back to 1636, when John Cook sold it to Thomas Cook. An 'open trestle post mill' standing on a frame, it could be moved to face the wind by the 'tail pole' at the rear. This could only be done by the unassisted strength of the miller and his assistants, which inevitably limited its size.
The early windmill at Silverley may well have looked like this. Acquired by the Cambridge Preservation Society in 1932, it is open to the public on certain days. (*Cambridgeshire Collection, Cambridge Central Library*)

Hobson's Choice

Thomas Hobson was a pioneering entrepreneur. His father, also called Thomas, was a carrier in Cambridge in 1561, taking goods and people by horse to London and other places. In his will Thomas (senior) left his son 'the team where that he now goeth with, that is to say the cart and eight horses and all the harness and other things thereunto belonging'. Thomas ran horses between the George Inn in Trumpington Street, on the current site of St Catherine's College, and the Bull Inn in London's Bishopsgate, transporting goods by cart and wagon and supplying barrels of live fish to the Royal Court.

A pioneer of the hire industry, Hobson was the first person to hire horses. His death in 1631, at the age of 86, was said to be caused by enforced idleness because a plague outbreak had prevented travel. During his lifetime Thomas became well known for business acumen: to ensure that his horses were neither overworked nor underworked, he hired them in strict rotation. No customer, no matter how wealthy or important, received preference, but had to take the first horse stabled by the door, giving rise to the expression 'Hobson's Choice', meaning 'that or nothing' or 'take it or leave it'.

Thomas Hobson, Cambridge's pioneer entrepreneur, who gave rise to the expression 'Hobson's Choice'.
(*Cambridgeshire Collection, Cambridge Central Library*)

Gas and steam power

George Bower of St Neots was a leading figure in the history of the gas industry. Born in Lincolnshire in 1826, at the age of 24 he bought an ironmonger's shop in St Neots Market Square and patented a coal gas system which could power up to 5,000 lights. He began making domestic gas cookers; by the age of 30 he had established the Vulcan Gas works in St Neots and was setting up urban gas supplies. He provided lighting for over 1,000 British towns and such exotic places as the Viceroy of Egypt's palace. However, George overexpanded himself by taking over a Brazilian steamship company which collapsed. He lost £130,000 and his fortunes never quite recovered, yet he still managed to start afresh, patenting the Bower-Banff process for coating iron and steel with magnetic oxide. Companies wishing to install the Bower-Banff process often had to use workmen from the Vulcan works. His US associates said that the St Neots workmen who came to build a furnace in Brooklyn were the finest they had seen, even though the man in charge (having been born before the 1870 Education Act) could not read or write.

The River Cam's high lime content at Sawston has caused the village to become a centre for tanning and papermaking. Edward Toogood, from a St Neots family of papermakers, introduced steam power to Sawston. By 1840 his Sawston factory had become one of the country's leading paper manufacturers. From 1819 the Evans family established control of Sawston's leather industry. Thomas Sutton Evans insisted that his employees used only shops and pubs owned by him, and even tried to regulate churchgoing. In 1897 his opponents established the Eastern Counties Leather Works and broke his tyranny. Fortunately his descendants were more enlightened, and Evans and Son and the Eastern Counties Leather Works continue to operate.

Chivers, the jam-makers

The Chivers family made an important contribution to the food industry. Stephen Chivers, a descendant of Huguenot refugees, was a farmer at Histon who grew fruit for sale in Yorkshire. In 1873 there was a glut of fruit, so his sons, William and John, suggested that

The first Chivers jam factory, in a barn on the family farm in 1873.
(*Cambridgeshire Collection, Cambridge Central Library*)

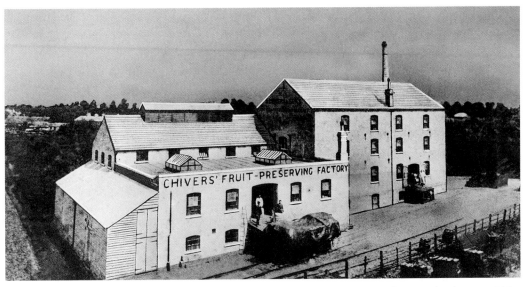

The Chivers jam and fruit-preserving business grew rapidly, as shown by this photograph taken in 1888.
(Cambridgeshire Collection, Cambridge Central Library)

The filling room at the Chivers factory. (Cambridgeshire Collection, Cambridge Central Library)

they make jam to the recipe of a relative who was a cook at Pembroke College, and they hired some cooks from the college for the purpose. This was so successful that the family closed their Yorkshire depot and opened the Victoria Works in Histon to make jam, followed by marmalade and other processed fruits.

The Chivers family stood at what was then the cutting edge of modern technology: they claimed to be the first English industrialists both to can fruit and to generate their own electricity to power their factory. At the turn of the twentieth century they set up laboratories and employed chemists to improve their products. Charles Lack, the works engineer, invented automatic filling machinery and vacuum caps. The microbiologist Mamie Olliver, working at the Chivers laboratories, discovered the high vitamin C content of blackcurrants, initiating their use in cold remedies.

The Chivers family introduced an early profit-sharing scheme in 1891 through which more than a third of the workforce were 'co-partners' by the 1920s. The family also started advisory committees to maintain consultation and dialogue with the workforce, and were among the first employers to institute a subsidised canteen and health care. William Chivers died prematurely in 1902, leaving John to manage the business. By John's death in 1929 the company was employing 3,000 workers and producing 4,600 tons of jam a year. After the Second World War, like many British companies of the time, Chivers neglected to install modern machinery and equipment. In 1959 it was incorporated into the Schweppes and then the Cadbury-Schweppes groups, yet within this organisation the Chivers brand name remains synonymous with jam and related products.

Fenland woad

Woad production is a lost Fenland industry. Woad was once used in textile manufacture as a source of indelible blue dye. In the thirteenth century it was grown at Over, and St Ives and Winchester fairs were the only places from which it could be exported from England. In the sixteenth century indigo began to supersede woad dye and by the nineteenth century cultivation was confined to the Fens. There it was revived by Robert Peel, who used woad dye to colour the first police uniforms.

Woad (or 'Wad' as it was called in the Fens) was last grown commercially at Parson Drove. The seeds were sown like corn, but the plants required constant weeding. In June the leaves were plucked and crushed in a woad mill, a circular building with turf walls 3ft thick. Three wheels, each weighing 1¼ tons, turned on axles by horses, crushed the leaves. The resulting pulp was then rolled into 2ft balls, which were left to shrink to a quarter of the original size and then dried for three months. They were next taken to a couching house to be heated and fermented in water for between two and six weeks to form a paste. This had to be done in complete darkness, so workers were locked in the couching house until the process was finished.

Waddies (as woad workers were called) had to be paid well for this demanding task, especially since fermenting woad had an unpleasant smell. Woad exhausted the soil after four years, so the industry was peripatetic: mills and buildings used to make the dye were constructed so that they could be disassembled and moved as required. The labour-intensive nature of woad dye production made it expensive, and, since 5lb of indigo from India could create as much dye as 2cwt of woad paste, the market inevitably shrunk until it was killed off altogether by an unexplained crop failure in 1914.

Woad worker and horse at Parson Drove woad mill. (*Cambridgeshire Collection, Cambridge Central Library*)

Waddies (woad workers) and woad mill at Parson Drove. (*Cambridgeshire Collection, Cambridge Central Library*)

Arthur Jarvis, the last Parson Drove waddie, died in 1970 aged 90. The industry is commemorated in local names: Woad Farms at Parson Drove and Tydd St Mary and the Woadman's Arms pub at Newton.

The Cambridgeshire Coprolite Rush

Although Cambridgeshire is not normally thought of as a mining area, there have been two mining ventures here. Robert Millicent, a London apothecary, inherited a heavily mortgaged estate in Linton in 1734. In an effort to restore the family fortunes he brought some Yorkshire miners to Linton to dig for coal, despite the fact that there is no evidence of coal deposits anywhere in Cambridgeshire. By Robert's death in 1740 a 225ft shaft had been dug, the deepest and most unproductive excavation in the county's history.

Coprolite mining was the county's most significant nineteenth-century industrial development. The Cambridgeshire coprolite bed, running between Guilden Morden and Burwell, is a greensand deposit of fossilised dinosaur remains laid down about 110 million years ago. Twelve miles wide, between 15 and 20ft below ground level, it is normally a foot thick, increasing to 4ft in places. (Ironically the thickest and potentially most profitable deposits lie below Cambridge itself, where mining was impractical.) In 1829 William Buckland found that greensand deposits contained phosphate. Surmising that they were fossilised dinosaur excrement, he called them coprolites from the Greek *kopros* (dung) and *lithos* (stone), though subsequent analysis has suggested that, while they contain animal waste, they consist mostly of organic remains. About twenty years later it was realised that the phosphate content gave it excellent potential as fertiliser.

The 'Cambridgeshire Coprolite Rush' began in 1855 with the discovery of deposits under Coldham's Common, probably by labourers digging for brick clay. The Cambridge Corporation leased areas to diggers, quietly overruling by-laws obliging them to maintain the common as public land. Over seventeen years nearly all the common was dug: the Corporation used the profits (over £1,200 in 1857 alone) to finance public building works such as Cambridge Corn Exchange and Fulbourn Hospital. Private and corporate landowners followed suit. St John's College financed the lavish rebuilding of its chapel from coprolite extraction on its estates (a dubious benefit, as the college's medieval chapel was needlessly demolished in the process); the discovery of coprolite below glebe lands financed many church restorations (a blessing proportionate to the reader's opinion of Victorian church restoration).

Landowners generally leased land to contractors for mineral extraction, usually with the agreement that it would be returned to agricultural use afterwards. Pits were therefore dug in strips to make refilling easier. Minerals had to be separated from the soil. At first they were washed in pits, but mechanisation eventually became common. Extracted material was placed in a circular drum about 30ft in diameter and 10ft high, which was filled with water from a pump and stirred by a horse-drawn beam. It has been suggested that these separation pits gave rise to stories of treacle wells made famous by the Mad Hatter in *Alice In Wonderland*. Separated minerals were transported to factories to be broken down in furnaces and mixed with sulphuric acid to make fertiliser. The Cambridge Manure Corporation was established in the city in 1855, with a windmill for grinding coprolites, but later moved to Duxford, probably because of easier rail access.

Plan of a coprolite washing mill, an industrial plant that is said to have given rise to stories of 'treacle wells'. (*Author's collection*)

Coprolite diggers at Orwell. (*Cambridgeshire Collection, Cambridge Central Library*)

Coprolite deposits contained many fossils; university academics and students paid a shilling or more for good specimens, and fossil stalls were set up on Market Hill. Some landowners inserted clauses into mining contracts giving them the right to keep fossils. The University Museum of Geology contains 10,000 specimens found during the coprolite mining rush, which are among its most scientifically valuable exhibits.

It is difficult to estimate the number of people that were employed by the coprolite industry, since work could be seasonal and peripatetic, but 600 diggers were said to have come to Reach Fair in 1869. The 1871 census for Bassingbourn showed 180 coprolite diggers in a total population of 1,700. In Burwell, with 2,000 inhabitants, 66 men dug coprolites and 108 worked in a coprolite factory. It seems fair to say that in some villages the coprolite industry employed between a quarter and a third of the adult male population. A digger could earn £2–3 a week. Some social commentators complained that much of this was spent on drink, and it was not coincidental that some coprolite merchants owned pubs: the 1871 census showed the Bird in Hand on Cambridge's Newmarket Road (near Coldham's Common) licensed by James Swann, who employed eighty diggers. But some workers used their wages to improve living standards, and boasted that they were no longer dependent on farming, where weekly wages were a mere ten shillings or less.

During 1875 and 1876 over half a million tons of coprolite fertiliser were produced in Cambridgeshire, selling at £2 8s per ton. But the economic depression of 1877 and the

developing US chemical fertiliser industry caused a spectacular slump: in just one year production dropped to 70,000 tons, and prices fell to £1 8s per ton. There was a brief revival when an area near Cambridge's Huntingdon Road (now the site of New Hall College) was developed, permitting extraction of the thick Cambridge deposits, while in 1888 Lady Francis, a Fen Ditton landowner, provided work for local unemployed men digging coprolites on Quy Fen. But by the 1890s the few remaining coprolite fertiliser manufacturers were running at a loss, and the last factory closed in 1898. Production briefly revived during the First World War, when the phosphate was used to make munitions, but the return of peace dealt the industry its final, fatal blow.

Among the few visible traces of the industry, there is a weighing house on Coldham's Common, now a cottage; parallel ridges and hollows can be seen on the grass behind this, indentations left by coprolite diggings; unfilled coprolite pits can also be found on marginal land at such places as Quy Fen. The coprolite mining boom was of undoubted historical significance, being the first example of large-scale open-cast mining in Britain and the world's first artificial fertiliser industry. There are plans to erect a public sculpture of coprolite in Bassingbourn, a one-time centre of the industry.

The headquarters of the Cambridge University Press. Sometimes known as the Freshers' Church, because it is said that its appearance and Gothic decoration has led many new students at Cambridge to mistake it for a church, and that other students have even tricked them into going there to attend Sunday services. (*Author's collection*)

Paper-making and publishing

Cambridge University has inevitably created a demand for books and their production. John Siberich set up the first printing press in Cambridge in 1521, and Henry VIII granted the university the right to print and sell books in 1534, making Cambridge, Oxford and London the only towns in England allowed to do so.

With books came the need for paper, and Fen Ditton was home to the second paper mill in England (after one that opened near Hertford in the 1490s). Started by the Bishop of Ely, Thomas Thirlby, it was in operation by 1557, with technical knowledge provided by Remigius Guidon, a papermaker from Lorraine. It closed before the end of the century, although the area is still called Paper Mills.

The Cambridge University Press Bookshop at the corner of Market Street and Trinity Street.
(*Author's collection*)

Cambridge University Press was formed in 1584, and is the oldest continually functioning publishing house in the world. It now prints 1,500 new books and over 200 journals on academic and educational topics each year, as well as the Authorised Version of the Bible and the Church of England's *Book of Common Prayer*. Governed by a syndicate of university members, it is not a company but part of the university, which receives its profits.

Concorde's droop nose during assembly at the Marshall Aerospace workshops in Cambridge. *(Reproduced courtesy of the Marshall Group of Companies)*

The Cambridge University Bookshop at the corner of Market Street and Trinity Street has been the site of a bookshop since 1581, the longest occupancy of a site by a single retail business in the world.

Space ventures

Cambridgeshire's leading companies include the Marshall Group, which was founded in 1909 by David Gregory Marshall, providing chauffeur-driven cars from a Cambridge garage. Twenty years later the Marshall family opened an aerodrome, which moved to its present Newmarket Road site in 1937. Here a programme was devised that could teach people with no previous flying experience to become a pilot and flight instructor in fourteen weeks. During the Second World War 20,000 pilots, one sixth of the RAF's operational strength, trained at Marshall's Aerodrome, whose programme was adopted as the basis of the force's present training course.

Now Britain's largest privately owned aerospace company, the Marshall Group was commissioned to develop Concorde's droop nose, possibly the world's best-known refinement of modern aircraft design. The firm also worked with Lockheed Martin to develop the Pegasus satellite launch vehicle, which carried the ashes of *Star Trek* creator Gene Roddenberry into orbit, bringing Cambridgeshire's industrial ingenuity to intergalactic prominence.

9 HEAVENS BELOW

Throughout history people have tried to improve their lives, and those of others, by adopting a communal lifestyle, sharing experiences and possessions with those of similar inclinations. It could be argued that this led to the foundation of Cambridge University, but other forms of communal living have also been started and exerted their influence in Cambridgeshire.

The Little Gidding Community, an attractive and inspirational social experiment, was initiated by Nicholas Ferrar. Born to a wealthy London mercantile family in 1593, Nicholas was deeply religious from his youth. Like many young aristocrats, Nicholas entered adulthood with a Grand Tour of European cultural and intellectual centres, when he visited both Protestant and Catholic religious communities and studied medicine at Padua. Returning to England, Nicholas rose in London society, impressing James I with his eloquence, but in 1624 he decided to seek a spiritual life. With his mother Mary he bought a country estate at Little Gidding, where he was joined by his brother and sister John and

Susanna and their families, to follow Christian life as described in chapter two of the *Acts of the Apostles*.

Little Gidding had been depopulated after the Black Death, and the only buildings there were a ruined church used as a barn, the manor house and a shepherds hut. After rebuilding the church the Ferrars adapted the Manor House into an oratory, writing over the door, 'Flee from evil and do good and dwell for evermore'. They rose early to maintain a daily rota of services, eating two meals a day before retiring to sleep at 9 p.m., although Nicholas and other members often spent a nightwatch reciting psalms or singing quietly. The Ferrars worked on a 'Harmony of Gospels' with the aim of conflating the four gospels into a single narrative. They instituted the 'Little Academy' to read and discuss historical and spiritual texts, and planted a physic garden to prepare free

Nicholas Ferrar's grave in front of the west door at Little Gidding Church. (*Author's collection*)

Little Gidding Church, rebuilt by the Ferrar family as the centre of their community in remote countryside west of Huntingdon. Its rural setting still conveys an atmosphere of serenity. (*Author's collection*)

medicines for local people. A dovecote was converted into a school, where three teachers taught English, Latin, mathematics, writing and music, with running, vaulting and archery on Thursday and Saturday afternoons. At one point 100 local children attended, receiving a penny from Nicholas for every psalm they learnt. John Ferrar's wife, Bathsheba, was a dissenting voice: resenting Nicholas's control of the family she was often uncooperative.

George Herbert was Vicar of Leighton Bromswold, and worked with the Ferrars in renovating the parish church in contemporary style: it retains one of England's best seventeenth-century church interiors. Nicholas published George Herbert's writings after his death in 1632; they became, and remain, very popular.

When Nicholas died in 1637 some printed works were burnt on his grave to show that his worldly life had perished, and his brother John took over the community. Charles I had visited Little Gidding in 1633: in 1640 John and his eldest son, also called Nicholas, presented the King with a copy of their Gospel Harmony. Both Charles and young Nicholas suffered from stammers: the king offered advice on overcoming this difficulty and offered to sponsor young Nicholas's career, but, sadly, the youth fell ill and died a few weeks later. Charles I visited the Ferrars again in 1642, when preparing for the Civil War, and in 1646 after his defeat. Realising that the Roundheads would suspect Little Gidding as a place where the King might hide, John smuggled him to a cottage at Coppingford, but Charles was captured a few days later. John and his sister Susanna both died in 1657; Bathsheba immediately returned to the London she sorely missed. The Ferrars continued to live at

Little Gidding. John's eldest surviving son, also called John, restored the church in 1714, and his descendants maintained it, but the intense spiritual regime faded away, and the hall burnt down early in the nineteenth century.

In the twentieth century T.S. Eliot visited Little Gidding, after which he named the last of the poems that make up his *Four Quartets*. Alan Maycock formed a friends group to perpetuate Nicholas Ferrar's memory. This led to the formation of the Little Gidding Trust, which bought Manor Farm, a Victorian farmhouse near the church, and renamed it Ferrar House. Here a renewed spiritual life is pursued.

Glass roundel in Little Gidding Church showing Nicholas Ferrar's last words: 'It is the right, good old way you are in; keep in it.' (*Author's collection*)

The Little Gidding pilgrimage, 4 December 2005. (*Author's collection*)

Thorney was home to a large community of Walloon Protestants from Flemish areas of modern Belgium, which was under Spanish rule in the seventeenth century. During the sixteenth and seventeenth centuries Protestantism spread among a substantial minority of the population of France and Flanders. Both French and Spanish governments subjected these converts to arbitrary and harsh treatment, and many fled to England, hoping they would be allowed to practice their religion in a Protestant country. French Protestants were traditionally known as Huguenots (although this is now a suspect term, as several different forms of Protestantism were followed in France), while Walloons were, strictly speaking, not French. The staff at the Thorney Museum, which maintains displays on the Walloons' achievements, now prefer to call them 'Strangers' (a contemporary term for foreign Protestant arrivals) or apply the more modern name of 'Settlers'.

Thorney Abbey Church, restored in 1639 for use by Walloon Protestant settlers in the area. (*Author's collection*)

Many Walloons had experience in draining and cultivating marshland. Their abilities were appreciated by Francis Russell, the 4th Earl of Bedford, and Cornelius Vermuyden – the English aristocrat and Dutch engineer who organised the draining of the Fens. Some settled at Whittlesey before being offered a home (and exemptions from tax) on the Earl's estate at Thorney. In 1639 the Earl signed an agreement with the Bishop of Ely that the remains of Thorney Abbey Church could be restored as a church for the settlers, where services could be held in French.

Walloon Huguenots who had helped to drain the Isle of Axholme near Doncaster lived at Sandtoft in Lincolnshire, where they found themselves subject to great hostility and animosity from neighbouring English communities. After their church was ransacked in 1653 nearly all the Sandtoft community migrated to Thorney. Ezekiel Danois, a native of Compiègne who had preached at Boulogne before fleeing to England to escape persecution, became their minister and was a popular figure at Thorney for twenty-one years. Over the following seventy years four further French and Walloon ministers officiated at Thorney, the last, Charles Le Seur, dying in 1744.

In 1657 a further group of Protestants from the Calais region settled at Parson Drove. In the 1740s William Cole found families at Thorney who still spoke French in private conversation, and met Henry Pujolas, the minister at Parson Drove, a small man in his nineties who still spoke with a strong French accent. The Thorney Settlers kept a separate parish register between 1654 and 1727: births average twenty-nine a year for the first decade and thirty-eight for the second decade, suggesting a total community of between 500 and 1,000. During the eighteenth century they lost their separate identity as they were absorbed into the surrounding English communities.

Like many refugees, the French and Walloon settlers did not leave their homeland because they believed life would be easy in England; they were compelled to flee in terror and poverty from an arbitrary government who persecuted them for their personal beliefs. At Thorney and Parson Drove they brought new life and prosperity to the communities. They made a crucial contribution to the reclamation of the Fens, introducing the French or paring plough to the region, and the cultivation of coleseed: a cash crop which could be grown on land that was too damp for cereal cultivation or pasturing animals. Their story demonstrates that refugees and other immigrants bring many resources, skills and benefits with them.

The Manea Colony was founded in 1838 by William Hodson of Upwell, an ex-sailor who had become a farmer and Methodist lay preacher, partly inspired by Robert Owen, the industrialist and pioneer socialist, and with support from James Hill, a Wisbech merchant and radical. William Hodson bought 200 acres of land adjoining the Bedford Level at Manea. (Coincidentally, when Cornelius Vermuyden began draining the Fens Charles I had suggested building a new town called Charlmont at Manea. It is not known if William was aware of this.)

Believing that all social evils were caused by class divisions, William adopted the motto 'each for all'. Everybody would work together to build houses and manufacture goods. Food would be grown, prepared and eaten in common, while machinery would be operated for everybody's general benefit to reduce labour. He planned to heat houses by flues from a central fire, which would be safer, healthier and more economical than allowing separate household fires. All matters would be decided by vote, in which women

Print of Manea Colony. Published by the colonists themselves, it probably shows an idealised view of the settlement. Note the horse-drawn railway. (*Cambridgeshire Collection, Cambridge Central Library*)

would have an equal say to men, a truly radical idea for the time! There were complaints that the first colonists, who arrived on Christmas Day in 1838, were lazy, undisciplined and prone to drunkenness and riotous living; but these soon left, and in 1839 William made a new start with a new group of people, who took the name 'Communionists' and called their settlement Cambridgeshire Community Number One. They published a journal, the *Working Bee*, which announced plans for a truly egalitarian society and described activities at the colony, possibly in an idealised way (articles read like Virgilian pastoral idylls, and make little mention of the dampness and remote nature of Fen life). It was claimed that over 100 Communionists had put 136 acres to agriculture and planted 1,000 fruit trees. Bricks were made from clay dug on the colony, while a horse-drawn railway transported materials around the site. Some houses and a windmill were built, together with a communal kitchen, refectory and library, while a printing works was set up. An observatory was topped with a flagpole flying a tricolour above a Union Jack to symbolise conquered tyranny.

Communionists shared duties according to their abilities and capacity, all eating the same food and abstaining from alcohol. They were paid in 'labour notes', which could be exchanged for supplies in the colony stores. There was organised leisure with cricket, bowls and dancing, and evening classes. A uniform was adopted: a tunic, trousers and hats for men, and dresses for women. A boat, the *Morning Star*, was acquired, in which the Communionists sailed along the Bedford Level. There were plans to start a factory to build agricultural machinery. William Hodson made lecture tours to promote the colony (which began to attract more visitors than it could accommodate), and his daughter was born there on 27 June 1840, the first birth in the community.

After a good harvest in 1840 events took a turn for the worse: the Communionists found no buyers for their produce, while James Hill, their Wisbech supporter, went bankrupt. William Hodson and the Communionists began arguing, sometimes quite violently, about how best to continue with the venture. Cambridgeshire Community Number One collapsed, and William Hodson emigrated to America. A farm on the site retained the name Colony Farm: after the First World War it was purchased by the government, who created 3-acre smallholdings for ex-servicemen there. Parts of the colony continued in use as farm buildings (a farm on the site was called Colony Farm until the 1970s) but these have all now vanished. There are no longer any remains above ground at Manea, though there is a fascinating model of the colony (with working components and a taped commentary) at the Octavia Hill Birthplace Museum in Wisbech.

Some of Cambridge University's most attractive informal social gatherings converged on the Lord Nelson pub by the ferry at Upware. From about 1850, when Tom Appleby became landlord, the Lord Nelson became a popular rendezvous for vacationing students. Two University clubs, the Society of Idiots and the Beersoakers, met there during vacations, engaging in sports during the day and drinking and general merriment at night. Club rules

Richard Ramsay Fielder, the 'King of Upware'.
(*Cambridgeshire Collection, Cambridge Central Library*)

The Five Miles From Anywhere, No Hurry pub at Upware. (*Cambridgeshire Collection, Cambridge Central Library*)

(probably issued in a spirit of levity) said nobody should say what he meant on pain of forfeiting a quart of ale, although 'club' may be too formal a description for what were habitual social gatherings.

Richard Ramsay Fielder was a popular Upware figure. Born in 1823, he graduated from Jesus College in 1851 and moved to Upware, where he was known for his loud costume of scarlet waistcoat and corduroy breeches. He frequently carried an earthenware tankard, inscribed with 'His Majesty's Pint', filled with rum punch, which he shared with lightermen. It was later recalled that he would fight all comers, led nightly revels and was called King Of Upware. (It is unclear if he underwent a mock coronation or if the title was simply conferred by popular assent.) As the Lord Nelson became popular it acquired a new name, the Five Miles From Anywhere: No Hurry. Some regulars claimed that the name continued So Don't Spill or even There's Nowhere Else To Go. It is often said that Richard Ramsay Fielder invented the name, but the honour was claimed by other habitués, notably Edmund George Harvey, a future Rector of St Mary's Church at Truro.

Between 1852 and 1856 a student group, the Upware Republic Society, met there. Arthur Gray, a local journalist, donated the Republic's Visitor's Book to Cambridge University Library. Activities included boating, wildfowling and skating. Among the members were Samuel Butler, a future author, and James Clerk Maxwell, who was to become a leading scientist.

Years later, when former members were asked about the Republic in the early twentieth century they thought it had dissolved with the passage of time and the annual movements of the student population. Richard Ramsay Fielder eventually left Upware, and died in

Folkestone in 1886, apparently in quiet respectability. During the First World War German prisoners of war were kept in the Five Miles From Anywhere and left it semi-derelict, with most of the windows broken. Having closed as a pub, it burnt down in 1955. A modern pub with the same name has since been built on the site. Although this bears no resemblance to the Victorian building the memory of Richard Ramsay Fielder and the Upware Republic's halcyon days continues to hold out the romantic appeal of lost student life.

The Papworth Village Settlement for tuberculosis sufferers was one of the world's great advances in health care. At the start of the twentieth century tuberculosis, or TB, disabled many people, and caused one eighth of all deaths, including one third of deaths among men aged between 15 and 44 and half the deaths among females aged between 15 and 24. Dr Pendrill Charles Varrier-Jones, a Welsh Cambridge graduate, became the Cambridgeshire tuberculosis officer in 1914 when aged 21. Pendrill had the idea of forming an industrial colony for TB sufferers, where they could be rehabilitated, either by being trained or retrained in the necessary skills to maintain themselves, or, if their condition proved incurable, by working at the colony. In 1916, with the support of Professor Clifford Allbutt, a Cambridge medical academic, Pendrill bought a house at Bourn, where he established the Cambridgeshire Tuberculosis Colony with fourteen patients and two nurses. Fresh air was vital for TB sufferers, and patients made their own accommodation in the form of wooden shelters with shuttered sides.

By 1917 Pendrill had acquired sufficient funds to buy the Papworth Hall estate at Papworth Everard, where patients maintained carpentry and shoemaking workshops, and ran poultry, pig and fruit farms, a jewellery workshop and a printing works; patients were

TB patients' huts, Papworth Colony. (*Cambridgeshire Collection, Cambridge Central Library*)

A patient at the Papworth Colony working on a Kirby glider during the Second World War.
(Cambridgeshire Collection, Cambridge Central Library)

paid trade-union rates for their work. By 1930 the Papworth Colony had an annual turnover of over £68,000. Showrooms were opened in Cambridge and London to advertise and market the colony's products. Not wishing to separate the permanently disabled from their families the Papworth Village Settlement was created where patients could make permanent homes. Eight cottages were bought in 1918, and over the next twenty years more than 100 were built, mostly by patients. Papworth was self-governing and self-supporting; patients were admitted on the understanding that they would behave and 'do the right thing'. The colony provided its own entertainment, running a pierrot troupe, holding dances and showing films; Cambridge academics came to give lectures. The colony attracted the interest of the royal family, who were regular visitors.

Pendrill, who was knighted in 1931, died ten years later, aged only 58, having helped to establish similar colonies for TB sufferers at Pearmont in Ireland and for ex-servicemen at Preston Hall and Ensham in Kent. During the Second World War the Papworth Colony produced aircraft parts. By then 350 TB sufferers were employed there, while 200 patients

were housed locally with their wives and families: all children born in the settlement were free of the disease. After the war Papworth Hospital joined the National Health Service, when a coach-building works was set up, making ambulances, mail vans and Green Goddess fire trucks.

In 1952 a cure for TB was discovered, but the lessons and experience acquired could be used in other areas, and from 1957 the hospital began working with people suffering from other disabilities. This new side to its work expanded. As the Papworth Trust it now promotes choice and independence for people suffering from physical disabilities across Eastern England.

Queen Mary and Princess Margaret with staff and patients at Papworth Colony.
(Cambridgeshire Collection, Cambridge Central Library)

10 What's in a Name?

Place names often reveal much about a region's history, while linguistic change can sometimes create odd or amusing verbal constructions. Cambridgeshire is the only county in England named after a bridge. The name Cambridge first appears in 875, when the *Anglo-Saxon Chronicle* described how Vikings camped at Grantabrygg. This is the earliest reference in Anglo-Saxon literature to a standing, manmade bridge, the first built in Britain since Roman times. At the furthest navigable reach of the Cam, on the only route where an army could cross from East Anglia to the Midlands, it has been suggested that King Offa of Mercia, ruler of most of central England between 758 and 796, had it built to promote commerce and demonstrate his power. The bridge was rebuilt several times in wood; a stone bridge was not built until 1754. In 1823 this was replaced by a metal bridge designed by an engineer named Arthur Browne, and cast partly in Derbyshire and partly in a nearby riverside foundry run by the Finch family on land now occupied by St John's College. By 1969 modern traffic regularly congested the bridge, making it unsafe, and the local authorities planned to demolish it. Fortunately it was saved in 1972 after a public outcry, and modern traffic use is now restricted.

The present Cam Bridge at Cambridge. Scudamores has hired out punts on the Cam since 1910.
(*Author's collection*)

The market places at Cambridge, Huntingdon, St Ives and Chatteris are called Market Hill, the Cambridge street leading off the market is called Peas Hill; the area between Great St Mary's Church and the University's Senate House is called Senate House Hill, and another nearby street is called St Andrew's Hill. None of these are on particularly high ground: here 'hill' meant an open area. Since Peas Hill was the site of the Cambridge fish market until the twentieth century, it has been suggested that the name derives from *pisces*, the Latin for 'fish'. However, pease pottage, a mixture of peas and grain, was a stable food into Tudor and Stuart times, and it is possible that this may once have been an area where peas and similar foodstuffs were sold.

Petty Cury, leading off Market Hill, is a unique street name, derived from a mixture of (rather poor) medieval Latin and French words for 'Little Kitchen'. Fourteenth-century

Petty Cury before modern development. (*Cambridgeshire Collection, Cambridge Central Library*)

spellings include (in rather bad Latin) *Parva Cokeria* and (in French) *Petite Curye*. Most large medieval towns had a Cook's Row where cooked food was sold. Cambridge may have possessed two or more such streets, or one divided into sections, the larger of which may have changed its name or been cleared away. Petty Cury was once an interesting section of Cambridge's town centre, containing a row of historic shops, inns and business premises but in 1973 the more historic side of the street was demolished.

In Cambridge there is a unique custom of referring to areas of open public land as 'pieces'. Cambridge's Anglo-Saxon market place was called Sale Piece. Standing north-east of the original Roman settlement on the north of the Cam, Sale Piece passed out of use after the castle was built in 1068 and has long since vanished. But the use of the name has continued, most obviously with Parker's Piece and Christ's Pieces to the south of the city centre. Parker's Piece is named after Edward Parker, a college cook who rented it from Trinity College. In 1613 Trinity College exchanged this with Cambridge Corporation for £50 and land elsewhere (including the site of Nevile's Court and the Wren Library). It became a popular venue for cricket and football games, and thus it seems appropriate that the city's modern public sports centre and swimming pool was built on the south side of the plot. Christ's Pieces are so-called because they lie behind Christ's College (although the

Feast on Parker's Piece, when a dinner was held for 15,000 people to celebrate Queen Victoria's Coronation. (*Cambridgeshire Collection, Cambridge Central Library*)

land is owned by Jesus College). Areas of The Backs behind King's and Clare Colleges are called Scholar's Piece and Clare Hall Piece. An open field in the Petersfield area was acquired as a public space in 1898 and called St Matthew's Piece (from the Victorian St Matthew's Church nearby). The Corporation had said it was to be for the people's recreation in perpetuity, but sections have since been built on and a residents group is now trying to save it from further development.

Before the discovery of St Ivo's supposed remains in AD 1000, St Ives was known as Slepe, but not because there was anything tired about the place: the word means 'muddy', probably referring to the river bank. (The modern word 'slippery' derives from a similar root.) A street called Merryland bisects St Ives Market Hill; the name does not refer to any happy or enjoyable activity that occurred here, but probably derives from Mary's Land, Mary in this case being the Virgin Mary. The Waits is a riverside street whose name comes from the Anglo-Saxon *wiht* meaning 'to bend', referring to a bend in the River Ouse. A street running parallel to the market is called Tenterleas, probably derived from cloth production: cloth on a loom was stretched on tenterhooks (hence the expression 'to wait on tenterhooks'). It is believed that the area was given over to the weaving, bleaching or sale of cloth. Great and Little Farthing Close were built over a field that had the same name in the eighteenth century, probably because it was divided into four areas. Pig Lane is the only road in the county named after this animal. In 1971 St Ives police station was built there. Amazingly, nobody made the connection before the station was opened between the street name and the use of the animal name as an offensive slang expression for a police officer, and the address became something of a national joke until the section of the road containing the station was renamed Broad Leas.

March derives its name from the Old English *Mark*, meaning boundary, probably because it stood on the border between marsh and dry land. Robingoodfellow's Lane is one of March's longest roads. In the eighteenth century it was a country track and in 1730 a pot containing 160 Roman silver coins was discovered here; perhaps it was thought to be a fairy's secret treasure.

Whittlesey means Witel's Island; like many fen communities it was an island in a marsh. It contains several unusual street names. It is uncertain why Gracious Street in the town centre should be so-called. The staff at Whittlesey museum said that people who lived here may once have held unusually devout religious beliefs, although there is no certain proof that this was the case. Other odd names are more easily explicable: Bassenhally Road is derived from the Anglo-Saxon *baesten healh*, the nook by the lime trees. Snoots Road derives from *snote*, a point of dry land reaching into water, in this case Whittlesey Mere, a lake that was drained in the 1850s. Snoots Common at Stretham is named from a similar peninsula. Drybread Road is said to be so named because it led to the town workhouse!

Some place names are quite literal. Ely means Eel's Island: eels were very common in the Fens and Ely was taxed for 3,750 eels a year at the time of the *Domesday Book*. Thorney means an island where thorns grew. Fowlmere is named from a large mere where wild birds abounded. Much of this was drained in 1854, but the remaining part now forms a very attractive and important nature reserve and bird sanctuary, thus maintaining its original role. Foxton, nearby, means 'fox's tun', a farm where foxes could be found. Snailwell is also appropriately named: it does not mean that snails were found here, but that there was a slow stream here, and the River Snail which rises here is indeed quite slow. However,

Westley Waterless does not refer to any lack of water. Instead it derives from a mispronunciation of 'Water leys', meaning water meadows: land deliberately flooded to assist agriculture.

Some place names were terms of disparagement or ridicule. Hatley St George was once known as Hungry Hatley. It may have stood on poorer soil than the neighbouring parishes of East Hatley and Cokayne Hatley: Hungry Hill at Westley Waterless and Hungry Hall Cottages at Wyton may have been named because they stood on marginal land. Two Cambridgeshire parishes and several smaller settlements are called Caldecote, derived from 'cold cottages', meaning either cold in the literal modern sense, or just poor and uninviting; even now they are small and remote settlements. Coldharbour, in Knapwell, Over, Whittlesey and Guilden Morden, probably means 'remote corner'. Coldham's Common at Cambridge derives from the same root, though, paradoxically, the discovery of coprolite deposits here initiated a nineteenth-century economic boom in the county. Gorefield probably derives its name from the Old English gor, meaning 'marsh', rather than implying that any blood that was shed there. Grunty Fen (well known locally as the home of Dennis of Grunty Fen, a personality who appeared on BBC Radio Cambridgeshire) does not sound like the most beautiful place. This may be the case, as the name derives from grumen, a word meaning 'shallow', 'low' or 'muddy', thus Grunty Fen was named as a shallow muddy area.

Other names have more positive connotations. Guilden Morden means Golden Hill, and may have been regarded as rich or beautiful; in Anglo-Saxon times Peterborough was called The Golden Burgh on account of the abbey's magnificence. Glatton means happy or pleasant tun or farm. Yaxley derives from the Anglo-Saxon geace's ley, meaning 'cuckoo's clearing'. Cherry Hinton, a village that has now nearly merged into Cambridge, was just called Hinton until Elizabethan times; the prefix Cherry is said to have been added for the rather obvious reason that cherries were grown here, perhaps an early form of market gardening.

Curiously one village name predates a modern personal name. The popular girl's name Wendy was invented by the author J.M. Barrie for a character in his children's story Peter Pan. By pure coincidence (and quite unknown to J.M. Barrie) a Cambridgeshire village called Wendy predates Peter Pan by several centuries. The name derives from a bend in the River Cam, which, to use atrocious poetic phrasing, makes a wending course in the river.

Norman Cross, where the Great North Road (the modern A1) joins the road to Peterborough (the modern A15), has always been a well-known location, even if there is no proper village there: in the Napoleonic Wars there was a large camp for French prisoners-of-war here, and long before this it gave its name to an Anglo-Saxon hundred (or administrative region). It could be thought that William the Conqueror or his Norman followers erected a cross here, but the region was known as Norman Cross before 963, over a century before the Norman Conquest; evidently it was named from Norsemen, Vikings who could have settled here in the ninth or tenth century.

Drove is a common name for roads and even settlements in the Fens. Droves are causeways that stand above the Fen marshes, so-named because cattle and other animals could be driven along them. Parson Drove is one of the earliest uses of this name, being so-called by the fourteenth century. Adventurers' and Undertakers' Fens or Lands are also common names. The reclamation of the Fen marshes from the seventeenth century was a risky enterprise that required the deployment of vast resources at great expense. When initiated it was not certain that the project would be successful. Landowners and entrepreneurs who backed the reclamation were therefore known as Adventurers, because they ventured their money in the scheme, often in return for a share of the reclaimed lands, which were thus called Adventurers' Fens. Undertakers' Lands are named from the engineers who undertook to reclaim areas of fen.

Several Fenland parishes, including Cottenham, Elm, Haddenham and Soham, contain areas of land called the Lots. Land here was divided up, and villagers were allocated areas to cultivate by the drawing of lots. Fen Lots at Whittlesey derives its name from the same process.

Roads called Honey Hill at Fen Drayton, Fen Stanton, Gamlingay, Gorefield, Paston and West Wratting are in marshy areas, and the name may refer to the muddiness and stickiness of the ground. A street on sloping ground in Cambridge is also called Honey Hill, possibly because it was once a muddy street. Frog End at Great and Little Wilbraham, Haslingfield, Shepreth, Frog's Hall at Bluntisham, Frog's Abbey at Coveney and Frog's Abbey Lane at Wimblington may be so-called because of the marshy nature of the land. Bogs Gap Lane at Steeple Morden is a similarly low-lying area. Cawdle Fen can be found near Ely, and there is a Cawdle Ditch at Fulbourn. This name means 'cold spring' or 'cold stream'. Lazier Fen at Stretham may derive its name from the word *leys*, meaning pasture or meadow. Joist Fen (which gives its name to Joist Farm) at Waterbeach may derive from the word *agist* meaning 'to take in livestock', as cattle may have been pastured here. Hinge Farm can also be found on Joist Fen: the first name might just be a humorous extension of the second. Yen Hall at West Wickham derives its name from the Anglo-Saxon *ean*, meaning 'lamb', suggesting that sheep or lambs were kept here.

An area north of Manea is called Bedlam, giving its name to Bedlam Corner, Bedlam Bridge and Bedlam Farm. It is uncertain why this was so-called. Bedlam was a medieval variant of the name Bethlehem: after medieval monks began to care for people with mental difficulties at Bethlehem (or Bedlam) Hospital in London the name became a general word for insanity. Possibly this area of Manea was called Bethlehem by a religiously inclined landowner (a nearby farm is called Chapel of Ease Farm); on the other hand it may be a sarcastic term, meaning that only a lunatic would wish to live there.

The Dog In A Doublet at Thorney gives its name to one of the most important fen drainage schemes. In the sixteenth century hunting dogs often wore little waistcoats or doublets, and this became the expression for a particularly brave or daring dog (and thus a brave huntsman). This popular Elizabethan expression has survived in this now unique pub name.

Some woods have unusual sounding names: Castor Hanglands is so-named as it stands on a slope, 'hangings' being a word for a hillside. Sounds Plantation at Chippenham is probably a corruption of 'sand', named after the sandy soil it grows on. Rice Wood at Helpston derives its name from *hris*, the Anglo-Saxon for 'brushwood'. Salome Wood at Leighton Bromswold is not named after the Biblical dancer, but derives its name from *sealh*, the Anglo-Saxon for 'willows'.

Some farm names are puzzling. Powder Blue Farm at Eye is named after a powder once used in laundry, but nobody seems to know why. Nor does anybody seem to know why Malice Farm at Thorney should be so-called. Now lying semi-ruined and derelict at a remote end of Thorney, it lives up to its name.

Ditton Docks is a name which passed into local folklore. Once, if Cambridge people were asked where they had been and they did not wish to answer, or regarded this as something that the questioner had no right to know, they would reply 'Ditton Docks'. Ditton in this case refers to Fen Ditton, now a suburb of Cambridge. The answer may seem amusing in the twenty-first century, when nothing larger than a houseboat is seen on the Cam at Fen Ditton. In fact, until the nineteenth century the Cam was navigable to Fen lighters and barges, which carried goods between Cambridge and the Fenland ports, such as King's Lynn and Wisbech. A staithe (landing area) at Fen Ditton was used by small boats, particularly for trade at Sturbridge Fair. Thus Fen Ditton did possess a dock, although the concept of a dockyard was a humorous example of rhetorical hyperbole. To improve upon the joke, the tower of Fen Ditton parish church is clearly visible from the staithe, and humorists referred to it as the local lighthouse! Another example of rhetorical hyperbole was applied to a landing point at Horningsea, a few miles further upriver, which was called Horningsea Pier.

The Pits at Isleham sounds like a dreary address. It is a literal name, being a former quarry, yet in 1841 there were over seventy dwellings here, housing over 300 people below normal street level. At the start of the twentieth century there were forty houses and two

'Ditton Docks', a waterside area at Fen Ditton, jokingly referred to as a dock; the church tower in the background was sometimes described as a lighthouse. (*Cambridgeshire Collection, Cambridge Central Library*)

The Pits at Isleham. (*Cambridgeshire Collection, Cambridge Central Library*)

The Great Whyte at Ramsey. (*Author's collection*)

pubs here. Most have now been cleared away, but there are still some houses on the former quarry floor and its sloping sides – among the county's few hillside dwellings.

Ramsey's main street is called Great Whyte, and a road leading off it is called Little Whyte. These were originally quays built alongside a tributary of the River Nene, and the name probably derives from the Anglo-Saxon *whit*, referring to a bend in the river. The tributary was covered over in the nineteenth century, but still runs under the road surface.

The road leading north out of Soham is called the Shade; it adjoins Shade Common. Yet this has always been open land and is not at all shady. It is probably so-called because a Shade was also a name for an area of land in the middle of a common.

The entry to Ghost Passage at Wisbech. (*Author's collection*)

Street sign at the entry to Quidditch Lane, the Cambourne street that attracts Harry Potter fans from a wide area. (*Author's collection*)

Ghost Passage is a long passage running off Wisbech's central Crescent. This mysterious and sinister name may derive from the fact that several chapels stood nearby and their burial grounds backed onto the passage.

When the new town of Cambourne was built west of Cambridge its name did not win universal approval. Many people thought the town should have been called Monkfield, after the field it was built on, which was so-named because it was owned by St Neots Priory. It was felt that Monkfield represented continuity with the past and moreover gave the town a unique identity: there is already a town called Camborne in Cornwall, but there is no other town or village called Monkfield. One street in Lower Cambourne has acquired unexpected fame, as it was called Quidditch Lane from a ditch that ran alongside it. This was an archaic name for a dry ditch. Quite coincidentally, in J.K. Rowling's famous books about the boy wizard Harry Potter, one key feature is a game called Quidditch, a favourite sport among wizards. The popularity of the Harry Potter books has grown so rapidly that most of the UK population has acquired some knowledge of their contents. As this happened Quidditch Lane began to appear in the national press and attract visits from Harry Potter fans. Local residents have taken this unexpected attention in good sport (to use another pun), and houses in the road have been given names from the Harry Potter books, such as Muggles (a wizard term for ordinary humans who lack magical powers), The Golden Snitch and The Quaffle (after items used in the game of Quidditch). Another house in Quidditch Lane is called The Owlery, a reference to the owls which also feature prominently in the books. When a contest was held to name two newly created lakes nearby, the chosen names were Whomping Willows and Sirius after some unconventional trees and a character in the books.

11 CALENDAR CUSTOMS

Seasonal customs have enlivened the passing of the year in Cambridgeshire. While some have faded away with the passage of time, others have been maintained or revived, while new traditions continue to evolve. Plough Monday, the first Monday after the twelfth day of Christmas (6 January), was traditionally regarded as the last day of the Christmas holidays, when the men and boys of a village would pull a plough around the village streets, stopping at houses (especially the largest houses where the wealthiest people lived) to ask for money. People not paying might have furrows drawn across their front garden or doorstep. Some celebrations included the initiation of boys who had helped with ploughing for the first time the previous autumn, either by putting on a heavy shoe into which nails were hammered, or by having their faces rubbed on a horse's bottom.

In Cambridgeshire Molly dancing often enlivened Plough Monday. A team of villagers, usually six or eight, performed dances accompanied by a musician. Early references mention a hurdy-gurdy, but by the nineteenth century this had been replaced by a violin or concertina. Dancers wore a white shirt and a hat which was often decorated with ribbons. They hung a sash, decorated with rosettes, over their shoulder, tied more ribbons around their elbows and wrists, and leather straps around their knees, then painted their faces black. One man would be dressed (usually rather unconvincingly) as a woman. Again, they performed before houses so that the occupants would pay them, or in the hope that passers-by or spectators would give coins, and a collector often accompanied them, carrying a receptacle for donations. Participants normally divided the money raised between themselves, but in some instances they may have bought groceries for elderly villagers.

The Revd William Cole's diary records how, in 1768, local boys came to his home at Waterbeach drawing a plough, with bells on their clothes and their faces painted black, to dance to the accompaniment of a hurdy-gurdy. In 1840 six men danced at Godmanchester: three were in their 80s, two were in their 70s, and one was a mere stripling of 65; all put straw down their backs and carried brooms. (It has been suggested that this was to give them the appearance of witches, although this is not certain.) It seems that William Cole was witnessing a well-established custom, and even the oldest dancers at Godmanchester had no knowledge of its origin. Nobody thought of naming the practice until 1866, when the expression 'Molly dancing' was coined, and this by outsiders. A Moll or Molly was a name for a man who dressed like a woman (for whatever reason). If this has stuck it is simply because nobody ever thought of an alternative.

Molly dancing also took place on Boxing Day, and sometimes continued for a few days after Plough Monday, when dancers would not only perform in their own community, but also in neighbouring parishes. It took place in Peterborough, but residents of Cambridge and Huntingdon are never known to have danced: perhaps they thought of themselves as townsfolk or city dwellers. However, villagers from the west and south-west of Cambridge often met on Cambridge's Market Hill on Plough Monday to dance against each other, before returning to their home villages for further dancing at night. Molly dancing continued at Linton into the 1920s, and at Little Downham in 1931 four villagers danced around Ely and Littleport accompanied by a musician and a collector, though this team gave their last performance in 1933.

Plough Monday celebrations may have fallen out of favour owing to a general and possibly exaggerated belief that they encouraged drunkenness and riotous behaviour, even what might now be called 'demanding money with menaces'. Their decline accelerated during the twentieth century as the rise in wage levels and living standards, slight as it may have been, reduced the need to seek extra money, and as workers were drawn into non-agricultural forms of employment. The upheavals of the First World War also did much to weaken rural traditions. However, in some villages Plough Monday celebrations were encouraged. If a schoolteacher or a prominent local figure was sympathetic to traditional customs he or she might even organise them. At Swaffham Prior the schoolteacher organised the children in blackening their faces and drawing a plough around the village singing

> A sifting of chaff, a bottle of hay,
> See the poor crows go carrying away,
> Squeak by squeak they wag their tails,
> Hi nonney! Hi nonney!

Here and at Great Glinton, Earith and Warboys children continued to celebrate Plough Monday into the 1930s.

At Balsham as many as fifty men drew a plough around the village until 1936. They took the ritual quite seriously, even forbidding children to accompany them. It may therefore have been appropriate that this was the first Cambridgeshire village to reintroduce the practice. After a visit by the Cambridge Morris Men in 1951 some local people decided to revive Plough Monday the following January to raise money for charity. Having collected £17 16s 6d on that first occasion, they maintained the custom until 1956. A second revival began in 1972. A wooden plough was built using timbers from the barn where the original plough was housed. The sum of £65 was raised for the church restoration fund, and since then the celebration has continued every year. In 1977 the Cambridge Morris Men joined the celebrations to perform the first revival of a traditional Cambridgeshire Molly dance.

I attended the 2006 Balsham Plough Monday celebrations, which were a great success, despite not starting till after 6 p.m. (few people in Balsham now work in the village and a late start was necessary to ensure that most villagers were at home). The plough had been taken from its shed a few days beforehand so that damp would swell the timbers to make it firm. Participants turned out in appropriate dress, as ploughmen and agricultural workers; James Kiddy, a third-generation farmer, took the role of the Squire or 'Tommy', wearing a Victorian gentleman's suit and top hat. They were accompanied by the Cambridge Morris Men. Starting from Fox Road, a team of villagers walked the streets, some driving the plough or pulling it on ropes. The operation was taken sufficiently seriously that my offer to help draw the plough was rebuffed. Followers knocked on every door with the call of 'Pity the poor ploughboy'. There were regular stops for refreshments, and morris dancing.

The 1952 revival of Plough Monday at Balsham. On the left, wearing the top hat, is George Plumb, 64, the 'Squire 'or 'Tommy'. Next to him is Arnold Lambert, the 'Betsy'. The plough was over 200 years old. (*Cambridgeshire Collection, Cambridge Central Library*)

Plough Monday at Balsham, January 2006. (*Author's collection*)

It was impossible to keep modern influences away, as the rustically dressed ploughmen and ploughboys still coordinated movements by mobile phone! A small portion of the funds was kept to help finance the biannual village feast, which the ploughmen host, but the bulk of the money raised, totalling £2,267.60, was presented to the local branch of MAGPAS (Mid-Anglian General Practitioners Accident Service) and the air ambulance service.

Apparently Plough Monday was even used to settle old scores: an older resident said that in the 1950s an unpopular Balsham resident had his front garden ploughed up.

Plough Monday has since been reintroduced at Ely (although there it has been transferred to the second Saturday of January) and St Neots. In 1979 a newly formed dance troupe, the Old Hunts Molly, revived it at first at Graveley (with a service in which a clergyman blessed the plough) and in subsequent years at Fenstanton. In 2006 the ceremony was revived at Pampisford. This continued restoration of an important rural custom deserves praise and support.

There was no philanthropic basis to the rather less pleasant Plough Monday custom of 'mumping', when men simply demanded money with the menacing rhyme:

> Mump, mump, mump,
> If you don't give me a penny
> I'll give you a thump.

This could often get out of hand, and there can be little doubt that, on nights before street lighting, it could be quite frightening for an isolated person to be confronted by a gang of rough young men chanting this ditty. The practice was common among coprolite diggers – in 1870 mumpers were said to have terrorised Bassingbourn – so perhaps understandably this may have been less tolerated than many other rural customs, and there is no record of efforts to perpetuate or revive it.

The Whittlesey Straw Bear Festival is another important revival of a rural custom. At Ramsey and Whittlesey one or two men who had participated in the local Plough Monday celebration would be swathed from head to foot in straw, and walk around the streets. The custom is first mentioned at Whittlesey in 1859, when it took place on the day after Plough Monday, and at Ramsey from 1863, when it was held on Plough Monday. Throughout the year at Ramsey people would keep the best straw for the bear, which would normally be used to dress two men (although only one 'bear' is mentioned in some years). One bear was usually led on a rope to perform impromptu dances before various houses. On other occasions he knelt on his hands and knees and growled, while those accompanying him pretended to control him by pulling at the rope and tapping him with light sticks. Again it was hoped that occupants of houses where they stopped and passers-by would give coins. There is no report of any comparable custom elsewhere in Cambridgeshire, or in any other part of Britain. In 1909 Professor G. Moore of Sheffield University, a native of the Fens, wrote to the writer James Frazer to say that he had returned to Whittlesey after forty years' absence to see a man leading the straw bear around the streets on a rope, as he remembered in his childhood. Frazer included Professor Moore's letter in his compendious analysis of world folklore, *The Golden Bough*. The custom last took place at Ramsey in 1893, but in Whittlesey the straw bear continued to walk the streets until 1913. (Interestingly, Plough Monday was celebrated here until 1934.)

When there was a competition to name a new Whittlesey pub in 1975 it was decided to call it the Straw Bear. (Anne Burgess, the artist who painted the sign, dressed as a straw bear for the opening.) Two years later a local parade celebrating the Queen's Silver Jubilee included a straw bear model and a man swathed in straw. Brian Kell of the Whittlesey Society then suggested a proper revival.

On 12 January 1980, accompanied by morris dancers, Brian Kell danced in the streets of Whittlesey swathed from head to foot in straw. The festival has continued every year since then, although now, to attract a larger audience, it takes place on the second Saturday in January. One large bear, followed by a smaller bear, roams the streets, accompanied by a band. This is followed in its turn by teams of morris dancers, some from local primary schools, some of whom perform traditional Molly dancing with black faces. Since modern cereal straw can be brittle, oats are grown on a local allotment to provide a tougher material. In honour of the Plough Monday tradition (and local farming) a plough is also drawn through the streets of Whittlesey. On the Sunday after the Straw Bear Festival some further festivities take place. There is a plough-blessing ceremony in one of the churches (when the plough that was drawn through the streets is taken to the church). The straw bear is burnt that afternoon (after the occupant has extracted himself). One of the most enjoyable and colourful events in the national calendar of folk customs, it forms a highly entertaining weekend.

Villagers in the Wisbech area once made 'whirling cakes' on Passion Sunday (the fifth Sunday in Lent), which they called Whirling Sunday. The practice was mentioned in the *Gentleman's Magazine* in 1789. It still took place at Leverington in 1891, when Whirling Sunday was a traditional fair day. By then it was said that it commemorated an old lady who was making some cakes one Sunday when the Devil carried her off over the parish church in a whirlwind, although this story may have been invented to explain the custom.

At St Ives twelve children throw dice for Bibles every Whit Monday. In 1675 Dr Robert Wilde, a clergyman, left £50 to buy land, the rent of which was paid to the vicar and churchwardens of St Ives to fund an annual service in the parish church when six boys and six girls would cast dice for six Bibles, while the vicar prayed that God 'direct the lots for his glory'. After the service the vicar and churchwardens were to enjoy 'a comfortable dinner for themselves, with as much claret and sack as the remaining money will provide'.

The land bought to fund the practice, which came to be known as Bible Orchard, has now been sold, and the money raised invested. The local public library has been built on the site of the orchard. (It seems most appropriate that a library should be built on land that was once rented to buy books.) The feast is no longer held: the vicar now reads a short address and prayers. A hymn is then sung, after which the children throw the dice. This originally took place on the altar – could it have been an echo of the soldiers drawing lots for Jesus' clothes, as in Matthew 27:35? – but after a bishop objected the dice were thrown on a table in the church. Since Dr Wilde's will did not specify that the children had to have any denominational affiliation, three each now come from the local Roman Catholic, United Reformed and Methodist churches, and three from the parish church. Groups from each church compete among themselves; the two highest-scoring boys and girls are then drawn against each other, and the highest-scoring couple then throw dice to decide who wins a Bible. Each throws three times to see who can achieve the highest total, draws being settled by another throw.

May Day celebrations at Glatton in 1856, as drawn by Edward Bradley (aka Cuthbert Bede), a local clergyman. (*Reproduced from the* Illustrated London News)

May Day celebrations were popular, when children, especially girls, made garlands: wooden frameworks decorated with flowers into which they placed a gaily decorated doll. Edward Bradley, a Victorian clergyman who wrote extensively on local folklore, described how when he was curate at Glatton the garland was a 6ft-high pyramid, carried in a parade of village children wearing ribbons, led by a May Queen with two maids of honour. The procession finished with a mid-afternoon tea on the village green, after which the garland was suspended between two trees in the village street, and local youths played a game in which they threw balls through it. (This affair sounds so elaborate that it must have required adult help and supervision.)

By the end of the nineteenth century most May celebrations were more modest. Two, three or four girls might carry a small, handmade framework, which they showed to passers-by in the hope of a penny or some sweets. Sometimes they placed a garland on a tree bough, which was lowered when people passed by with an accompanying suggestion of a penny to see the doll. Collection of money normally stopped at noon. Sometimes the custom was called May Dolling or the May Lady. Garlanding continued at Swaffham Prior until 1960, partly under the auspices of the village school, and at Rampton until 1988, by which time the taking of money was forbidden.

May garlanding at Yaxley in 1916: these junior Red Cross workers were evidently raising funds to help sick and wounded servicemen. (*Author's collection*)

May garlanding in the soke of Peterborough. Although the girls cannot be precisely identified, the card is postmarked as having been posted at Barnack in 1907. (*Author's collection*)

Cambridge girls with May garlands. (*Cambridgeshire Collection, Cambridge Central Library*)

In parts of England there was a custom for people, especially adults, to skip with ropes on Good Friday. In Cambridge this took place on Parker's Piece. Men normally turned the ropes while women jumped. The occasion was something of a picnic: people might bring food, and stallholders sold refreshments. Its popularity declined between the two world wars, and only a few people turned up when it last took place in 1941. Men and women at Bartlow and surrounding villages skipped on the Roman burial mounds known as the Bartlow Hills on Good Friday, but this custom seems to have passed out of use in the middle of the nineteenth century.

Stilton Cheese Rolling is a relatively new custom which takes place on the May Bank Holiday. Stilton cheese was, in fact, manufactured in Leicestershire, but acquired its name through being marketed and sold at Stilton's Bell Inn. The village once owed its importance to its location on the Great North Road (now known as the A1). In the 1950s the road was diverted to bypass Stilton. In 1959 the landlords of the Bell and the Talbot Inns took advantage of this to roll a 'Stilton cheese' (actually a segment of a telegraph pole) along the road. Claiming to be reviving a historic custom, they had in reality invented the practice. Spectators joined in, and cheese rolling races have continued every May Bank Holiday ever since. The race was originally organised by the village's playgroup, but it became too large for them, and the Stilton Community Association took over in 1981. (The race was cancelled once, in 2001, owing to the foot-and-mouth epidemic, but that year it was staged on television's *Big Breakfast* programme.)

Stilton cheese rolling starts at noon after the village's May Bank Holiday celebrations which now include morris and maypole dancing, and the crowning of a May queen, along with a funfair and music. Teams are encouraged to wear fancy dress; in 2005 the theme was 'sixty years on', to commemorate the end of the Second World War, but costumes are generally left to the competitors' discretion (in 2006 one men's team dressed as monks).

Good Friday skipping on Parker's Piece. (*Cambridgeshire Collection, Cambridge Central Library*)

Competing cheese rollers outside the Bell Inn at Stilton, May 2006. (*Author's collection*)

Teams compete in groups of four to roll a cheese from the front of the Bell Inn to the Church Street crossroads. As in 1959 this is a wooden replica of a Stilton cheese. The races are held as elimination contests; two teams of four people compete, and each team member has to roll the cheese at least once during the race. The winner of each race is paired off against another until the champions emerge. There are now junior, men's and ladies' championships before a semi-final and final race. In 2006 twenty men's teams, eight ladies' teams and six junior teams competed. The race has attracted international competitors: between 2003 and 2005 the winning men's team, Lakonjic, came from Poland. In 1997 Stilton had been twinned with St Christol-lès Alès in the Cevennes area of France: fortuitously, in 2006 a visiting group from that village happened to be at Stilton on 1 May, so an England vs France race was also organised, which the French team won. The year 2006 was also marked by the first wheelchair race, organised by a local man; participants enjoyed this, and there are plans to bring further entrants from Northamptonshire to take part in this event. The prizes, predictably, are whole Stilton cheeses along with trophies.

A cheese-rolling team passing the Bell Inn, 2006. (*Author's collection*)

The Dyslexic Time Lords, the winning men's team at the 2006 Stilton Cheese Rolling World Championships. (*Copyright Stilton Community Association*)

There is a pea-picking custom at Sawston in July. In 1554 John Huntingdon left all his land in Sawston to his wife Joyce on condition that she sowed a 2-acre field called Lenton Field with white peas, from which every poor person in the parish could gather a combe (4 bushels) to sustain themselves. After Joyce's death his estate would continue to fund charitable enterprises in Sawston, including the cultivation of the pea field. There is no comparable charitable bequest anywhere else in Britain.

Pea picking at Sawston. (*Cambridgeshire Collection, Cambridge Central Library*)

Although the Lenton Field's location has been forgotten, 2 acres of peas continued to be grown on Huntingdon's Farm for the annual pea-picking day, which usually took place on a July day between 9 a.m. and dusk. The villagers assembled around the field, and when the parish overseer (later the village constable) called 'All on!' they rushed in to gather as much as they could. The village school finished lessons early on pea-picking day so that children could help their parents gather peas, and Sawston Village College followed suit until 1939. It was not uncommon for arguments and even fights to break out if people were suspected of trying to take too much. When Huntingdon's Farm was sold in 1922 sale particulars said the new owner had to plant 2 acres of peas annually for the villagers' benefit. After the farm was split up in 1989 the parish council paid a local farmer to sow 2 acres with peas.

In 1554 many people could have been in danger of starvation in winter, and a few sacks of peas might have made a vital difference to their diet and their chances of survival. (One story holds that John Huntingdon made the bequest after hearing about a woman who had been hanged for stealing some peas, although there is no proof that this was the case.) Few people in twenty-first century Cambridgeshire are likely to be quite so desperate for food, so gathering now starts at 3 p.m. The precise date is changed each year and only advertised at a few local venues, to prevent too many outsiders taking advantage of it, but it is still a popular and well-attended event, and the field is normally picked bare by the end of the day.

12 This Sporting Life

Some Cambridgeshire sporting traditions have achieved a widespread popularity. The Fens were the home of speed-skating, where winter races over frozen waterways became popular. Recreational skating originated in the Netherlands (*skate* is a Dutch word); its introduction to England was described by the diarist Samuel Pepys, a native of Cambridgeshire. It has been suggested that skating was introduced to the Fens by French and Walloon settlers at Thorney or Dutch workers on drainage schemes. In 1763 John Lamb and George Fawn of Wisbech skated 15 miles for a 10-guinea prize, John Lamb supposedly winning in 46 minutes. Races developed into elimination contests. Two barrels were placed half a mile apart and sixteen skaters were paired off. In eight preliminary races two contestants started on either side of one barrel: they raced to the far barrel and around it three times, covering 1½ miles. Winners continued to be paired off, until two finalists competed for the prize. It was thought that elimination contests allowed everybody to race under equal conditions, and judges tried to pair skaters whose times closely matched. Group races were never greatly enjoyed, as speed was often reduced when skaters crowded together, while slow skaters often used fast skaters as windbreaks.

Larman Register of Southery in Norfolk won a championship race at Welney in 1850 to become the first person generally recognised as Fen (and national) Champion. Four years

A Fenland skating race: the location is uncertain, but this picture conveys something of the spirit of these occasions. (*Cambridgeshire Collection, Cambridge Central Library*)

later he was beaten for the title (and a silver watch) by William 'Turkey' Smart of Welney, who established Welney as the great nursery of Fen skaters, and the Smarts as the greatest skating dynasty. A clayman by profession, the origin of his nickname is unknown, though it is commonly supposed to have arisen from the country that was Britain's ally in the Crimean War, which was being fought at the time. During February 1855 Turkey won eleven races and prize money totalling £55 15s; at any one time 8,000 people might have

'Gutta Percha' (left) and 'Turkey' Smart (right), both in their 60s, at their final competition which took place at Littleport on 15 February 1895. Skating a half-mile race, Turkey won in 2 minutes, 4 seconds – 3 seconds and 10yd ahead of Gutta Percha.(*Cambridgeshire Collection, Cambridge Central Library*)

come to see him race. Turkey's great rival was William 'Gutta Percha' See, another Welney man, whose nickname was derived from a rubber used to manufacture golf and cricket balls, then regarded as the toughest and hardest-wearing man-made material. Their prowess was something of a legend, although in the many races in which they competed Turkey nearly always won and maintained his supremacy until his retirement, with the approach of middle age, in 1867; he even won a mile race in Birmingham in 1881 by some 250yd.

Although Turkey Smart and Gutta Percha See held great and well-deserved reputations, there is uncertainty over their full ability as there were no agreed standards for monitoring races. Officials measured courses by pacing them, and the accuracy of reported times was sometimes doubtful. Racing under monitored and regulated conditions began with the formation of a National Skating Association in 1879, the brainchild of James Drake Digby, a Cambridge journalist who wanted to bring Fen skating to a national audience. Turkey's nephew, George 'Fish' Smart of Welney, aged 23, won the British Championship for £10 at Thorney on a measured 1½-mile course in front of adjudicators using regulated time-keeping equipment, although poor weather conditions meant that he only covered the distance in 6 minutes, 10 seconds. Over the next two winters Fish (so-called because he was an expert swimmer) won fifty-five races in a row, and a national 1½-mile race at Elstree in 3 minutes, 17·4 seconds; while he also ran a straight mile in 2 minutes, 40 seconds at Cowbit Wash in Lincolnshire – an unusual achievement, as it was uncommon to find a mile-long stretch of ice capable of supporting a person.

The National Skating Association divided skaters into professionals and amateurs. Anybody who skated for a monetary prize (or practical object, such as a watch or a joint of meat) permanently forfeited amateur status. Many skaters were agricultural workers who saw races as welcome opportunities to earn money when the weather put them out of work, and were therefore classed as professionals. Amateur racers tended to be gentlemen farmers and members of the upper or middle classes, who never achieved the fame or prestige of professional skaters. Fred Norman, a Haddenham farmer, won the first 1½-mile amateur trophy race in 5 minutes, 23½ seconds in 1880. However, NSA rules forbade races between professionals and amateurs, so no overall champion emerged.

In February 1887 Fish's 22-year-old brother James and Gutta Percha See's 24-year-old son George, known as 'Young Guttee' brought Fen skating to international prominence by competing against leading Dutch skaters at Slikkerveer in the Netherlands. Young Guttee won a 1-mile race in 2 minutes, 53 seconds and a 3,500-metre race in 5 minutes, 42·4 seconds (beating James by a fifth of a second and 5·6 seconds respectively, and establishing official world records, while Charles Tebbutt of Bluntisham won an amateur race. Fen skaters held an ice festival at Bluntisham to celebrate their triumph.

Fred Ward of Tydd Fen won the professional cup in 1900 – he was the first amateur to turn professional, after complaints that he had accepted prizes of a chicken and a few shillings. But the twentieth century ended Fen skating's glory days. Not only were winters generally milder, but competitions concentrated on figure-skating rather than speed-skating. Skating rinks were built across the country, drawing skaters and contests away from the open Fenland countryside. One modern Fen champion was Neville Young, a Wisbech builder who won many races between 1947 and 1962, even though he practised and trained in London.

The Bumps

The Bumps have been a feature of Cambridge life since the 1820s. As the Cam is too narrow for full-scale competitive racing, student rowers hold races in which they try to 'bump' or touch other boats. Boats start at measured intervals. A bump occurs if two boats or crew members touch; if oars met while still in the rowlocks; or when one boat overtakes another. Both boats then withdraw to the riverbank. In the next race any boat that has made a bump is moved one place forward. After four days the boat at the head of the final race is the overall winner. (Elimination contests, in which boats were permanently withdrawn on being bumped until one winning boat was left, never achieved the popularity of mass bumping races and ceased before the end of the nineteenth century).

The Bumps are also a great spectator sport. At one time people watched from boats or tubs on the river and followed the race with an unregulated free-for-all when they battled their way back to Cambridge.

The May Bumps at Ditton Corner in 1909: at that date there was a stadium on the river bank to allow spectators a clearer view of the action. (*Cambridgeshire Collection, Cambridge Central Library*)

Spectators at a bumping race, some of whom have taken positions in boats on the Cam. (*Cambridgeshire Collection, Cambridge Central Library*)

A May procession: winners of the 1893 bumping races. (*Cambridgeshire Collection, Cambridge Central Library*)

There are two Bumps races, the Lents, held during the Lent term in March, and the Mays, held in the May term, but in fact in June. Students (and the best rowers) tend to be distracted by academic commitments and the Oxford vs Cambridge Boat Race in March, and the May Bumps are more popular and keenly contested, not least because they begin after examinations. Teams are grouped into divisions. There are four men's and three women's divisions in the Lents and six men's and four women's divisions in the Mays. A preliminary 'getting-on race' is held to admit new teams wishing to enter for the first time. Boats start upriver from Cambridge, at the Baits Bite Lock at Chesterton, separated at 1½-length intervals, and row towards a point near the Chesterton footbridge, a distance of 2,400 yd for the lead boat and 3,300 yd for the final boat. Crews that make a bump traditionally decorate their clothes and boat with flowers and greenery from the riverside path, while those that make four bumps in a row are said to have 'won their blades' and fly a club flag on their final journey home. Any crew that is unfortunate enough to be bumped four times receives a wooden spoon. Movement between divisions is possible, as the first boat in one division also becomes the last boat in the next division (a 'sandwich boat'). The boat to lead the first division at the end of the race receives the title 'Head of the River', and its crew holds a celebration in which an old and decayed boat is burnt. Since about 1840 non-university teams have held a bumping race in July. It is now organised by the Cambridgeshire Rowing Association, which awards the Bumps Plate to the head boat.

Trinity College Run

Many students have attempted to run around Trinity College's Great Court while the college clock strikes twelve at noon or midnight (taking between 37 and 52 seconds). The Great Court is 400yd in circumference (the largest courtyard in Cambridge) but students

The Great Court at Trinity College. Students have often attempted to run around the court while the clock (on King Edward's Tower, to the left) strikes twelve, but only two are officially recorded as accomplishing the feat. (*Author's collection*)

follow the flagstone path around the inside of the court, a circuit of approximately 350yd. David Cecil (Lord Burleigh) made the first authenticated run, on 7 June 1927, in 42½ seconds. Succeeding as 6th Marquess of Exeter in 1956, he had become in the meantime a distinguished athlete and an Olympic medallist. A student named Gordon Jones made another authenticated run in 43 seconds on 21 March 1950. Olympic medallists Sebastian Coe and Steve Cram made the run for television on 29 October 1988, and completed the circuit in 46 and 46.3 seconds respectively. Unfortunately, the clock struck in 44.4 seconds.

The 1981 film *Chariots Of Fire* shows Harold Abrahams, the Cambridge undergraduate and 1924 Olympic medallist, played by Ben Cross, accomplishing the feat. However, this scene, which was filmed at Eton College, is dramatic licence, as Harold Abrahams studied at Gonville and Caius and never attempted the run. Midnight runs also take place, often as mass races after evening functions. Since runners often wear ordinary clothes and footwear, and as they may have been eating (and drinking) heavily, their performance often leaves much to be desired!

The Cambridge Rules

Cambridge University formulated the rules of association football (or soccer). Parker's Piece is a favoured venue for student football games. At the start of the nineteenth century most undergraduates came from public schools such as Eton, Harrow, Winchester, Shrewsbury or Rugby, which all had different rules over such issues as the size of teams and pitches, the definition of a foul and the right to physically hold onto the ball (or other players). In 1848 a group of undergraduates held a meeting in a Trinity student's rooms. Between 4 p.m. and midnight they worked out a set of mutually acceptable regulations, called the Cambridge Rules, which they printed and pinned to trees on Parker's Piece. None of the originals have survived, but many copies were made. Only about 250 words long, the rules allowed handling under certain circumstances, while rule three said, 'Kicks must only be allowed at the ball'! Leaving much to the discretion of umpires and team captains, they were nevertheless the first rules to be officially agreed by opposing players. When the Football Association was established in 1863 it adopted the Cambridge Rules, which in turn have been used by most football associations across the world.

World Pea-shooting Championship

Witcham stages the World Pea-shooting Championship every July. In 1971 villagers were running a fund-raising campaign to build a village hall. When the master of Witcham village school, John Tyson, confiscated pea-shooters from some pupils he had the idea of a championship contest. This has continued annually, raising money for the village hall fund. John Tyson died in 2003, and the champion now receives the John Tyson Shield.

Competitors are allowed to bring their own pea-shooters, which can be made of any material, but cannot be more than 12in long. Competitors are paired off and fire five peas, in alternate shots, at a target. (In the event of a tie players fire peas alternately until one conclusively wins or loses.) Winners are paired off again, the final four competitors shooting ten peas each, with the winner of the final contest being the Open Champion. There are separate contests for children aged under seven and over eight, and team events for groups of four players.

Competitor at the 1996 World Pea-shooting Championship at Witcham. (*Tom and Anne Wood*)

In 1994 and 1995 a competitor brought a pea-shooter with a laser-enhanced telescopic sight. This led to complaints that he was gaining an unfair advantage. Eventually Tom Wood, the chairman of the organising committee, had the idea of a separate class for modified pea-shooters, with such aids as tripods and sights. The contest attracts visitors from Europe and North America: in 1996 the overall champion was Dan Sargant of the USA. In 2006 the overall champion was a woman, Sandra Ashley of Sutton, a nearby Fen village. That year the contest was attended by reporters for an Indonesian television company and a Russian news channel. Evgeny Ksanzenko, a Russian cameraman, was quoted as saying, 'You English people are crazy. The people in Russia will love this.'

Costers' Race

A costers' race was once held in Cambridge on Boxing Day. Competitors pushed a coster's barrow from the Newmarket Road to the Swan at Bottisham and back. It is unclear whether the competitors were costermongers, or whether anybody who could obtain a barrow

A costers' race setting out from the Newmarket Road. (*Cambridgeshire Collection, Cambridge Central Library*)

could participate. Fifteen competitors took part in 1910, when Ben Warren came first, reportedly in 1 hour 44 minutes for a prize of £1 5s. In 1913 there were fourteen participants: Ben Warren again won, reportedly in 1 hour and 26 minutes, for a prize of £2 5s, beating a competitor called Ellis by four minutes. All those finishing the race received half a crown, and collections for Addenbrooke's Hospital were taken during the event. The last race took place during the First World War, after which the custom was abandoned.

King Street Run

The King Street Run in Cambridge originated in the winter of 1955/6. Some students from St John's were in the Criterion Bar (a long-closed pub) when they had an argument with some medical students over how many pubs you could drink in without having to relieve yourself. It was suggested that the assembled company should investigate this the following night in King Street, where there were then eight pubs (with two others around the corner in Hobson Street and Short Street). The medical students never turned up, but three off-duty Royal Navy sailors offered to join in. Amazingly, the three sailors (who had already had something to drink) and most of the students accomplished the feat. The event owes its fame in part to Jonathan Crabtree, a participant (and a future high-court judge) who recorded the occasion. Successful participants decided to inaugurate the run as a permanent event in university life, drawing up a constitution, designing a tie and appointing 'Stoker' Williams, one of the participating sailors, Life President. There are now only five pubs in

The King Street Run pub in Cambridge, named after the university students' tradition of running pub races along the street. (*Author's collection*)

King Street, (one of them called the King Street Run in honour of the contest, but the race has become something of a student tradition and is currently organised by Terry Kavanagh, the landlord of the St Radegund pub.

The Fenland Sport of Bandy

A winter sport known as 'bandy' originated in Bury Fen, near Ramsey, in about 1790. It is not dissimilar to North American ice hockey, although it developed quite independently. Played on a pitch between 150 and 200yd wide, with a goal at either end, players used curved sticks, normally of willow or ash, and a 3in ball of tightly woven cloth, later replaced by gutta-percha.

Bluntisham, Earith, Swavesey, Over, Willingham, Cottenham, Chatteris, St Ives, Godmanchester and Huntingdon all fielded bandy teams, but Bury Fen remained undefeated until 1890, when the game spread to London and the Virginia Water Club beat them by 8 goals to 3 in an away match. A National Bandy Association was formed in 1891, when the Bury Fen team toured the Netherlands, beating hastily convened Dutch teams, and subsequently played across Scandinavia and Germany. After the First World War bandy faded from memory in Britain, but grew in popularity in Scandinavia, Russia and even North America.

An International Bandy Federation was founded in 1955, when world championships were held in Sweden and Russia. It replaced soccer as Russia's biggest spectator sport in 1997, and the Moscow International Olympic Congress accepted it as a 'recognised' sport in 2001. If five more countries accept bandy it will receive full Olympic status. It would be a true first for Cambridgeshire if a sport originating in the eighteenth-century Fenlands becomes a twenty-first century Olympic sport!

The Bury Fen Bandy team, 1890. (Norris Museum, St Ives)

INDEX OF PLACES